# MATT TALBOT

# Matt Talbot

by Eddie Doherty

THE BRUCE PUBLISHING COMPANY
MILWAUKEE

Nihil obstat: JOHN A. SCHULIEN, S.T.D., Censor librorum
Imprimatur: ✠ ROMAN R. ATKIELSKI, Administrator, sede vacante
Archidioecesis Milwauchiensis
Die 28 Aprilis, 1953

TO FATHER JOHN OF PATMOS
BENEATH WHOSE BLESSING HANDS
SO MANY RESTLESS SPIRITS
HAVE FOUND PEACE

# PRAYER

## FOR THE CANONIZATION
## OF

# Matthew Talbot

O Jesus, true friend of the humble worker, Who hast given us in Thy servant, Matthew, a wonderful example of victory over vice, a model of penance and of love for Thy Holy Eucharist, grant, we beseech Thee, that we Thy servants may overcome all our wicked passions and sanctify our lives with penance and love like his.

And if it be in accordance with Thine adorable designs that Thy pious servant should be glorified by the Church, deign to manifest by Thy heavenly favors the power he enjoys in Thy sight, Who livest and reignest for ever and ever. — Amen.

100 days' Indulgence each time.

*Permissu Ordinarii Dioec. Dublinen., die 15 Junii, anno 1931.*

# Part I

# 1

ON A pitiful dry day, in the city of Dublin, in the year 1884, a seedy young workman with a hang-over decided to quit drinking.

His flesh was crawling with the need of alcohol. His throat was as parched as a long-neglected desert. His eyes were bloodshot and weary through searching the streets for the sight of a friend with a bob or a bottle. And his hands were shaking — even in the depths of his coat pockets. Yet he took the pledge.

And if things all over the world haven't been the same from that day to this, maybe Matt Talbot's decision had something to do with it. Who can deny that?

There was nothing remarkable about Matt — not then. And there was nothing remarkable in his taking the pledge. Nothing is easier to take — nor harder to keep. But, one thing leading to another, a sinner can call on a priest, and a sot can become a saint.

It was only after Matt quit drinking that he became remarkable in any way. It was only after his death that he became, not only remarkable and famous all over the world, but even an object of veneration.

Some day, in your parish church, you may see a queer statue — maybe standing near that of the Little Flower or St. Anthony or even St. Patrick himself. And then again maybe you'll not. The Church hasn't canonized Matt yet, and may never do so. But it permits him to be called "the holy servant of God"; and that is tantamount to calling him the "Venerable Matt Talbot."

If you do see the statue, though, you'll know it by the sleazy overcoat it will be modeling; the round and dented iron hat canted over one eye and jammed tight around the bald spot; the long, ragged muffler wound tightly about the scrawny throat; the bony bare knees staring out of the slits in the baggy, thin trousers. And for all anybody can predict to the contrary, he may be holding a glass of ale in his right hand (sculptors being as they are) and wiping foam off his tough little mustache with his left.

There never was a photograph of Matt. And nobody thought it important to make a death mask of his face. Yet all sorts of people have contrived to deluge us with so-called likenesses of him, each more appalling than all the others. The statue, if there be one, may be ugly too. Yet, should it be placed in any church, you will see women kneeling before it at all hours of the day and night; the ill-clad, ill-fed women of the well-oiled; the cheerless victims of the cup that cheers. And it is possible that prayers said before such a statue may save millions of American drinkers!

Matt was twenty-eight when he took the pledge. He had been drinking since he was twelve. He had been drinking steadily. His intimates insisted he hadn't exhaled an entirely sober breath in all that time, and referred to him as "a proper bowsie." That, translated, might mean a genuine boozer, one who was strictly a souse, a good two-fisted whisky drinker, a whining beer moocher or a wino, or simply a wisp of a man who could get lit — and then go out like a light — from a whiff of the bartender's towel.

In Matt's case it meant, apparently, a nice little gent who could drink all night without making a nuisance of himself, who could be pleasant to everybody, who could sing happily and never weep — "from the eyeball to the high ball, Sal-l-l-ty Tears!" — who could put in a good night's work with a glass in either hand, get up early the next morning, and get to work on time.

Matt never spilled a drink nor stinted a day's work on the job.

He took the pledge for three months, though he felt he couldn't keep it for three hours. He kept it forty-one years.

It wasn't his years of sobriety that led Rome to consider his claims to heroic virtue, however. What startled the Church authorities, and started the saint-making machinery, was the extraordinary life Matt led after he had swallowed his last sip of hard liquor.

The "life of the party" became a recluse. The jingled gent who squandered all his money on keeping jingled began to save every farthing for the foreign missions. The tepid and indifferent soul kindled into flames that set a dozen or more bright fires burning in a tepid and indifferent world. The slave of alcohol became the slave of Jesus and His immaculate Mother, Mary; and he bound his arms and legs, and his waist with heavy chains as a token of that willing bondage.

Some of the links in those chains were found embedded in his flesh the day he dropped dead on his way to Mass. Some of them had rusted. It was the links binding him to Mary and her Son that freed him from the chains of alcoholism. It was those links that gave him to Christendom as a possible patron of all helpless drunks.

He who had loved gay people, and lots of them, and gay music, and funny stories, and brave speeches, lived the last years of his life in a lonelier and more austere manner than many of the anchorites one reads about in old stories of the early Church.

He shut himself up, after working hours, in a cold, bare, dark, uncomfortable little room at 18 Upper Rutland Street.

He slept on a mattress made of rough wooden planks laid on an iron bed. He covered himself with a cotton quilt. His main food was stale bread, with a little tea and cocoa — mixed — stirred in hot water and allowed to cool before drinking. He ate kneeling. He read books kneeling. He prayed for hours kneeling. He sang hymns kneeling. And, kneeling, he wrote, on any scrap of paper handy, passages copied from the books he loved the best.

Whether he saw visions or not in that dismal, glorious room, or whether he sometimes wrestled with the devil, or worked miracles of healing, or performed other prodigies, is part of the mystery of the man. Nobody really knows.

The place is a shrine today, drawing pilgrims from all parts of the world, especially those who need someone like Matt — who had been through the gin mill of life himself.

One feels an atmosphere of peace in the room. And of wonder. And of years of grace. The feeling of mystery and awe is so palpable one instinctively lowers his voice when he asks a question, and has a hard time restraining himself from falling on his knees. (Should he succumb to this impulse, as many do, he will find a prie-dieu handy; and he may remain in prayer as long as he desires.)

There was nothing notable or unusual about Matt in his drinking days, except that he never told dirty stories or said very much about women. His sisters have said again and again, "Ah, sure, Matt was the purest of human creatures." It may be they didn't know their brother as well as they thought they did; but there were plenty of Matt's men companions who said the same thing about him — after he died.

There was nothing vicious about the man, nothing mean or petty. When he had money he spent it — with his friends. When he didn't have it he would get it by pawning his coat or his hat or his shoes.

He was like a lot of other young men of his day — and of the present day. He always managed to reel into Mass on Sunday, no matter how drunk he had been. He could swear as readily and as profanely as the next man when he was moved or excited. He didn't go to confession or Communion very often. He had been away from the Sacraments for three years or more the day he took the pledge. And if he remembered to bless himself when he got up in the morning that was all the prayers he said. Oh, maybe, once in a while, when he wasn't too plastered, he'd begin a Hail Mary before sneaking into bed.

He was the average man. The average — God help us — Catholic. Why God chose him especially, and no one else, to lead thousands of people into sobriety, and perhaps from sobriety into sanctity, is another mystery.

He wasn't at all handsome. He was not tall nor athletic. There was nothing of the movie hero in him. He wasn't an intellectual. He could read and write, but it was labor. He might have to think a while before spelling cat for you; and he might have to spell it twice before he was correct. His handwriting, even in his ripe years, was not quite that of a schoolboy learning the alphabet. (Yet he could devour the most abstruse books on theology and understand them!)

He hated school. He quit when he was twelve, and went to work. And, as he began immediately the serious business of keeping himself safe from snake bite, he never had any time for study. You could assure the lad there were no snakes in Ireland. And he would admit it. But he could argue — couldn't he? — that it wouldn't hurt man or boy to keep himself prepared, "just in case."

He was poor and weak and ignorant and unambitious. For half a century or so he never earned so much as a pound sterling a week. It took a world war to raise his wages.

Matt was born on May 2, 1856, in the city of Dublin, then the most English city outside of England. He was one of twelve children. His father, Charles Talbot, and his mother, who was Elizabeth Bagnal, were devout Catholics. Charles, a most sober man, was a foreman for the Dublin Port and Dock Board in charge of large quantities of liquor. His father and his grandfather had had the same job years before him; and evidently had won their employers' complete trust for themselves, else Charles might have experienced the same hardships that came to other Irish Catholics during the terrible long years of the Famine.

Matt had seven brothers and four sisters. He went to the Christian Brothers' school, but did not take it seriously. He escaped from it as often as he could.

After he took the pledge he began to frequent churches instead of pubs. He felt he had to have some place to hide himself, some place far away from the barmaids he knew, from the companions he liked, from the old life he had led.

If these churches were, at first, merely substitutes for his favorite barrooms, they became, in time, substitutes for heaven. There were marvelous companions there, if a man looked around him earnestly. There were saints there, and beautiful angels. Mary was there too — virgin maid and pitying mother. And her Son. And the Holy Ghost. And God the Father.

Beauty was there. And serenity. And absolute safety. And such happiness of soul it was hard to bear.

What a fool a man was to waste his God-given time in a barroom when he could spend it in prayer before the altar of God! What an ass a man was to sell his soul and his body to the devil of drink when he could drive a much better bargain with the One who would come to judge the living and the dead!

# 2

MATT quit drinking without the help of a doctor, without the aid of any sodality or group, without the connivance of any pill surreptitiously stirred into his coffee, without the assistance of any beadle or cop or jailer or judge, or the conscious co-operation of a single pal.

From the moment he decided to stop until the moment he died, say some of the little pamphlets written about him, his body begged continuously for liquor. He was what old-fashioned physicians called "a hopeless addict" — yet one who found not only hope but all the other virtues with it.

Modern doctors do not use such archaic language. They hold that alcoholism is a disease, and that it is not at all incurable. In fact, they claim that even the worst dipsomaniac can be remade, with help — and with some co-operation on his part.

The attitude of the righteous and the bone dry has changed since Matt Talbot's time. That there are elements of sin in it, and that weakness of will is involved, cannot be denied. But there is not now such a contempt for alcoholics as there used to be.

The husband and father who staggers home late every night, or doesn't come home at all, or is brought in by friends or by policemen or stretcher-bearers or by some undertaker's assistant, is no longer regarded as an unnatural monster. Rather he is considered a sick man, a victim, a captive of his own appetite, a patient in sore need of intelligent and decent friends.

There is a growing sympathy for alcoholics and a widening understanding of their problems. The law, of course, still picks them up and puts them away — unless there is an election day coming soon. But kindly doctors study John Barleycorn's lost ones now. Science and pity have erected hospitals for their care. And common decency and Christian energy have built societies or associations, such as Alcoholics Anonymous, to bring them back into the highway of constant sobriety.

Is it possible that Matt had something to do with this new feeling, with this modern movement for the regeneration of men and women — numbered in the millions — who have ruined themselves through drink, or are doing so now?

Matt had spent many waking hours polishing some bar with his skinny elbows, and them thrusting themselves out of the sleeves of his shoddy coat, if he had a coat on. The hours he spent, in later years, with his bare knees pressed against cold stone or rough damp wood, must have been in retribution.

Surely in his devoted evenings he had not forgotten his fellow alcoholics? Certainly, when he was drunk only with the mercy and the wisdom and the power and the love and the glory of God and Mary, he had interceded for all the children of chaos, for all the ruins on Rum Row?

Undoubtedly Matt had discovered he could get more intoxicated through the love of heaven than through any beverage. He must have learned, too, that he could intoxicate at least a part of the world with that delicious vintage, and that he could wean many poor bar flies with a taste of the strong drink he had found.

He must have understood that he could atone, at least in

part, for some of his wasted years, for some of his misspent nights, for some of the foggy Sundays when he "slept off a jag" during Mass. He must have realized he could make some reparation for his own indifference, and for those of his peers, the average Catholics whom God might, otherwise, be forced to vomit from His mouth.

Sir Jos. A. Glynn, Matt's first biographer, and the one all others must go to for information, tells us in detail how Matt stopped drinking. But he doesn't say a word about how, or why, the child started. Nor does he give any reason to account for Matt's becoming a constant drinker, an alcoholic.

One becomes a habitual drinker because he wants some sort of escape. He wants to flee from too much misery, too much bitterness, too much boredom, too much monotony, too little self-confidence, too crushing a blow to his pride, his love, his comfort, his self-esteem, or his sense of security. He is annoyed, afraid, humiliated. He is in despair. He is suspicious. He wants something — courage, joy, companionship, freedom, a sense of power, maybe only a feeling of equality.

But what could induce a twelve-year-old boy to become a habitual drinker?

Perhaps Friedrich Engels can give us a clue — the same Engels who, with Karl Marx and other sour thinkers, gave us the present scourge of atheistic communism.

In a book called *Ireland*, which claims to be "a documentary record" compiled and edited by James Carty, and which the visitor to Dublin can purchase in any one of half a hundred bookstores, there is printed a letter written by Engels to Marx on May 23, 1856 — just three weeks after Matt was born.

> In our tour in Ireland, [Engels says, writing merely as a tourist] we came from Dublin to Galway on the west coast, then twenty miles north inland, then to Limerick, down the Shannon to Tarbert, Tralee, Killarney, and back to Dublin — a total of about four to five hundred miles in the country itself — so that we have seen about two-thirds of the whole country. With the exception of Dublin, which bears the same relation to London as Dusseldorf does to Berlin, and has quite the

character of a small one-time capital, all English-built too, the whole country, and especially the towns, has the appearance of France or Northern Italy.

Gendarmes, priests, lawyers, bureaucrats, squires in pleasing profusion, and a total absence of any and every industry. . . .

Strong measures are visible in every part of the country, the government meddles with everything, of so-called self-government there is not a trace. Ireland may be regarded as the first English colony and as one which because of its proximity is still governed exactly in the old way, and here one can already observe that the so-called liberty of English citizens is based on the oppression of the colonies.

I have never seen so many gendarmes in any country, and the drink-sodden expression of the Prussian gendarmes is developed to its highest perfection here among the constabulary, who are armed with rifles, bayonets, and handcuffs.

Characteristic of this country are its ruins, the oldest from the fifth to the sixth centuries, the latest from the nineteenth — with every intervening period. The most ancient are all churches; after 1100, churches and castles; after 1800, the houses of peasants.

The whole of the West, but especially in the neighborhood of Galway, is covered with these ruined peasant houses, most of which have only been deserted since 1846. I never thought that a famine could have such tangible reality. Whole villages are devastated, and there among them lie the splendid parks of the lesser landlords, who are almost the only people still there, mostly lawyers. Famine, emigration, and clearances, together, have accomplished this. There are not even cattle to be seen in the fields. The land is an utter desert which nobody wants.

In County Clare, south of Galway, it is rather better, here there are at least some cattle, and the hills toward Limerick are excellently cultivated, mostly by Scottish farmers, the ruins have been cleared away and the country has a bourgeois appearance.

In the South-West there are a lot of mountains and bogs but also wonderfully rich forest growth, beyond that again fine pastures, especially in Tipperary and toward Dublin — land which is, one can see, gradually coming into the hands of big farmers.

The country has been completely ruined by the English wars of conquest from 1100 to 1850 (for in reality both the wars and the state of siege lasted as long as that). It is a fact that most of the ruins were produced by destruction during the wars. The people itself has got its peculiar character from this, and despite all their Irish nationalist fanaticism the fellows feel that they are no longer at home in their own country.

Ireland for the Saxon — that is now being realised. The Irishman knows he cannot compete with the Englishman, who comes with means in every respect superior. . . . How often have the Irish started to achieve something, and every time they have been crushed, politically and industrially. . . .

The landowners, who everywhere else have taken on bourgeois qualities, are here completely demoralised. Their country seats are surrounded by enormous, wonderfully beautiful parks, but all around is waste land, and where the money is supposed to come from it is impossible to see. These fellows ought to be shot. Of mixed blood, mostly tall, strong handsome chaps, they all wear enormous moustaches under colossal Roman noses, give themselves the sham military airs of retired colonels, travel around the country after all sorts of pleasures, and if one makes an inquiry, they haven't a penny, are laden with debts, and live in dread of the Encumbered Estates Court.

Conditions weren't any better in 1868, when Matt Talbot left school and got his first job, that of a messenger boy for the firm of Edward and John Burke, wine merchants and bottlers for the Guinness stout people.

In those days, by the way, the boss seldom paid in cash. He usually gave the employees checks or drafts, or slips of paper of some kind, that could be cashed at certain bars. The average foreman got a percentage of the money spent in the taproom after the bartender had kindly and graciously — and methodically — cashed the slips presented to him. If a man, or a boy, were foolish enough to go to a bank for his money, or to some barroom unknown to his foreman, he might not have another payday. And if he soberly decided to spend the

19

money for food, rent, clothing, taxes, books, or repairs on his
home — and none of it at all across the bar — the Lord help
him!

The workers were paid, usually, every Saturday noon. Therefore they had ample time to spend their money, generously, in
the foreman's pet pub. It is easy enough then, to see how Matt
might start drinking before he was out of his teens. But, you
may ask, why did he quit school and go to work?

Joseph O'Connor, in his latest book, *Hostage to Fortune*,
an autobiography, gives us a clue to this minor mystery.
O'Connor was born more than twenty years after Matt Talbot,
and the school he went to was not in Ireland but in England.
Yet the conditions he describes were much the same in Dublin
as they were twenty years later across the Irish Sea.

> The Catholic school [O'Connor says] was a makeshift of
> corrugated iron, attached to a makeshift chapel of the same
> depressing material. . . . That school was a trying place for
> Lizzie and me, two little Irish papists intruding on a crowd of
> English children, who had racial pride sung into them three
> times a day.
> "Rule Britannia! Britannia, rule the waves;
> Bri-tons never, never, never shall be slaves."
> The teachers made us sing the herrenfolk anthem and
> like it. They could not comprehend that we might not like it;
> nay, that we might have reason to hate. It is hard to blame
> them. England was then at her zenith. Money was pouring in
> from the far corners of the earth. Her word was law in all the
> chancelleries of Europe, and only Ireland was vexatious. And
> we, being Irish, were just in the right place to be indoctrinated
> with true British spirit. . . . I did gather that I had suffered
> a great misfortune in being born Irish and that I should thank
> God for the happy chance He had given me of learning how to
> live it down. All I brought away with me was a sense of disgrace
> and a vague notion that I should be ashamed of being Irish. . . .
> I was a pariah, a butt for the gangs, who rushed me into
> corners and harried me like young wolves . . . it lasted long
> enough to instil in my heart, at its most impressionable period,
> a deep, abiding, unreasoning bias. . . .

20

Matt Talbot undoubtedly learned something of the Catholic religion, the religion of love, in the Christian Brothers' school in Dublin. He undoubtedly learned, also, that Britannia ruled the waves, that there was little hope in life for any boy who was both Catholic and Irish, that there was nothing ahead of such a lad but unending work, unending poverty, unending drink.

There are many old men and women in Ireland today who are still distressed or angry or sad or bitter when they remember their school days.

Ah [one of them says], the hatred put into us in the schools was out of the devil's own cold heart! It took us years to exorcise it.

How well I remembered the day when I learned that, in the daily Mass we attended, we were supposed to pray for our rulers! The terrible outrage of it, I thought. The impossible thing God demanded of us!

"I'll not," I said to my mother. "I'll never pray for her."

Her, of course, was Victoria.

"You will that," my mother said. "You'll pray for her, and on your two knees, morning, night, and noon. You'll pray for your rulers. You'll pray for all your enemies and all that hate and despise you. That way you'll be praying for Ireland too, and for yourself as well."

It was the hard lesson to learn. That it was. But I learned it. I learned it well.

Perhaps Matt Talbot was a pariah too. Perhaps he also couldn't help feeling ashamed of being Irish. Perhaps he hated the English just as ardently as other boys of his age. We do not know that he did, however. We do not know that he hated anyone or anything.

Perhaps he too prayed for the rulers of England, from the time he went back to the Sacraments until the last prayer that went through his mind as he walked down Granby Lane to his death.

It may be suggested that the primary reason Matt quit school at twelve and went to work was to earn money for the family. If so, his intention misfired sadly. For in all his wet sixteen years he brought home one single shilling!

The habitual drinker does not contribute much, if anything, to the family's support.

It was only after he quit drinking that Matt was of any help to his father and mother — or to anybody else.

# 3

THERE are plenty of drinking places in Dublin. Some of them are small and humble rooms; some are spacious, gaudy, brilliantly lit, and as full of chromium as the most modern bar on this side of the ocean.

Matt Talbot's prayers have not closed up liquor stores or saloons or night clubs, nor stopped any individual from drinking what he will.

The drunkard, though as well preserved in alcohol as any other specimen, will never be placed in a museum. So long as nature produces alcohol, men and women will drink it.

But then, it is probable, Matt never prayed for anything like Prohibition. He must have realized that alcohol, made by God, was meant for man; therefore it must be good in itself. It could be used; or it could be misused or abused. His prayers, undoubtedly, were only for the wretches who "couldn't handle the stuff," who couldn't quit drinking once they started, who would stop only because of the lockup, the strait jacket, or the morgue.

23

There was nothing elegant about the pub or the "snug" of Matt Talbot's days. His favorite haunts were dirty little rooms with plenty of sawdust on the floor, upended kegs for stools, and a couple of planks for a bar — rough wood planed and sandpapered so it wasn't likely to put any slivers through a man's elbow or drinking hand or forearm.

Many a morning Matt waited an hour or more, in the cold and the dark — and in the chasm of a great thirst — for such a place to open. Then he might get the job of sweeping out the old sawdust and replacing it. That would get him a free pint, or more, from the barmaid who let him in.

Only a few people could be accommodated in these deadfalls at any one time, and usually the customers were regulars, men working or living in the immediate neighborhood, men of a type, men who became friends in their cups; souls set free, as it were, for a time, from the cares of the day, from the feeling of inferiority, from the sense of serfdom.

Men could talk to each other in confidence in any of these hidden retreats. Men could speak openly the things that were in their hearts. Men could sing here, even such songs as that concerning Napper Tandy and his dark view of Ireland:

'Tis the most distressful country that ever you have seen,
For they're hanging men and women for the wearing of the
    green!

Men could tell each other stories, or repeat them over and over again, to bolster themselves in their pride of ancestry, or in the history of their country, or in the eminent superiority of some of their statesmen.

The story about Daniel O'Connell — or was it Grattan, now, or poor Parnell — in his tiff with the English Disraeli. Matt must have heard it a hundred times, and repeated it as often to friends who might also have heard it before — but who liked it anyway.

"So this Disraeli, mind you, cast aspersions on the ancestry of the great O'Connell. O'Connell related to all the kings of Ireland, no less. O'Connell, he intimated, in his nice diplomatic

24

way, was the descendant of drunken swineherds. Bedad, that's
what he meant if he didn't say the words themselves. Swineherds. But was O'Connell put out? The devil a put.

"Up he rose, as polished and polite as a granite shaft, and
as hard to dent. No man, he said, could prove or disprove that
he did or did not come from ancestors who were swineherds.
Not if he attempted to go far enough back into history. Sure
Disraeli himself was an example of this.

"Could the gentleman disprove, for instance, that he was
not a lineal descendant of Judas Iscariot? He could not. He
could not disprove it to a living soul that knew him. And with
that O'Connell sat down."

Sometimes a "peeler," a military policeman, stepped in, to
wet his whistle, or perhaps just to look around. Sometimes
other strangers came in out of the night, to join in the singing
or the storytelling or the discussions of Irish rights, or to
buy a drink for all the lads.

And once in a while a strolling minstrel found himself in
such a friendly bar, and stayed the night, playing reels and
jigs as well as ballads.

There was a fiddler who gave so much of himself to Matt's
favorite pub one night, that Matt felt sorely obliged to treat
him to the best in the house. But Matt had used up all his
credit, and his friends hadn't a farthing in their jeans.

It was Matt's custom to give his pay, entire, to the barmaid
presiding over this particular place. Her task was to keep track
of the drinks Matt had, and to let him know when he had
drunk almost to the bottom of that sum — sixteen, or seventeen, or eighteen shillings, or whatever it might be. Then he
could either drink the balance or hurry out to the pawn shop
and come back with coins enough to prop up his sagging credit.

This night, in his exuberance, Matt had drunk up the last
of his shillings. And he had nothing to pawn.

Suddenly he had an idea. There was the fiddler's old violin,
stuck over there in the corner. Sure, any pawnbroker would
give four or five bob on that. Matt patted the fiddler on the
back, bade him drink hearty, and asked to be excused.

25

"I'll be back in a minute," he promised, "and it's cheer we'll have for the brave music you gave us."

When he remembered the incident — probably the next morning waiting for somebody to open up the place so he could get busy with a broom and idle with a pint — Matt determined that, come what might, he would somehow, some day, redeem that fiddle, find the fiddler, and make up to him, if possible, the time and the money and the prestige he had lost through Matt's drunken generosity. Do what he would, however, Matt never was able to find the fiddler, or to redeem the instrument.

Matt must have missed the companionship of his fellow drinkers almost as much as the drink itself, after he took the pledge. He must often have been tempted to return to his pet oasis just to hear the voices of his friends, the stories, the arguments, the songs.

Ironically enough it was these friends who closed the bar to him on that historic day in 1884.

It was a Saturday morning, and for the first time in sixteen years Matt had failed to get up in time either for his sawdust drink, or for work. He had had at least one too many the night before. He needed another one now, before he got out of bed. But there was nothing in the house.

He staggered out and walked toward the pub his friends would visit in a few hours. He took his younger brother, Philip, with him. He had no credit at the pub. Neither had Philip. He had no money. Neither had Philip. But he had friends. And so had Philip.

He and Philip stationed themselves on the corner, where they could scan two streets. Men with money in their pockets would be coming along soon, coming to the pub, coming to relieve Matt and Phil Talbot of the thirst of thirsts, the hang-over of hang-overs.

Ah, saints and angels! Wasn't it good to have friends, and them with shillings tumbling over one another in their pockets! Wasn't it heaven's own blessing to hear one of them say, "Whisht, Matt, don't be standing there like you were lost in the Sahairy desert, man; come in with me and a drink take for the blistering day it is and the chilly night it's going to be."

Matt's friends appeared, shortly after noon. But there seemed a hesitancy in them this day, a dubious look on their faces, a fine false heartiness in their voices, and a shut hand in each pocket where the shillings might be rubbing elbows with each other.

"Good day, Matt," they said.

"We missed ye, lad," they said.

" 'Tis nice seeing you, Matt," they said.

Not one of all those fellows gave Matt the chance to say, "I don't mind if I do." Not one of them, whom he had treated so often, even mentioned buying a drink, though most of them went directly into the pub. Others, more ashamed of themselves, or more inclined to devious methods of diplomacy, pretended they had errands just beyond the pub, or across the street from it, or around the corner.

It was plain to Matt that nobody was going to unhang his awful hang-over. It was plain also to Philip.

"Let's keep on waiting," Philip said. "Somebody will surely come along and say more than just 'good day to ye, Matt, and good night to ye,' as well. Wait until my friends show up."

Matt shook his aching head from side to side. He was cut to the heart, he said. He had learned a terrible lesson. He had come to an important decision. He had determined to take the pledge; and he would take it this very night.

"You can stay," he said. "I'm going home."

"It's too early," Philip objected. "Mother won't be expecting you. Dinner won't be ready. Might as well stay here as go any other place."

Matt went home.

His mother was startled. She looked from his face to the face of the clock, then back to his face again.

"It's you," she said. "So early!"

Matt used to come home only when there was nothing more

to drink. He used to stumble into the house and reel into bed long after midnight. Here it wasn't yet time for the midday meal, and he was home, and —

Mrs. Talbot looked at him again, wanting to be sure.

"And you're sober!"

It was an exclamation, almost a shout, almost a loud hurrah, and at the same time almost a complete and emphatic denial.

For the first time in many years, perhaps, Matt really saw his mother, and realized all the things he had made her suffer.

"Yes," he said simply. "I'm sober."

A long time after the meal had been disposed of and the dishes put away, he told her he was going to take the pledge.

This must have been more than a little shock to Mrs. Talbot. She had prayed for Matt all his life, especially during the years of his habitual drunkenness. She had felt that some day he, and the other boys too, would stop drinking and turn into fine sober men like their father. But to have it happen this way, without warning as it were, was disturbing.

"Go take it, in God's name," she bade him, her voice sharp, her eyes suspicious. "But not unless you mean to keep it."

Matt sighed. After all, why should anyone trust him? Why should she, of all people, trust him? How many times had he broken his word to her? He couldn't count all the times. How many times had he promised to reform, to bring his money home, and to help his parents instead of helping the barkeeper put his kids through school?

He went to the room where he and his brothers slept and dressed. He washed himself, brushed his clothes, combed his rough and disheveled hair, and put on a cap. This was to be no ordinary occasion. A man must look his best.

"I go," he said. "I go in the name of God."

It wasn't easy to talk like that. He had so often spoken that name lightly and with disrespect. He had used it even in anger. He wasn't much of a Catholic, he remembered. He went to Mass every Sunday, of course. But then he was supposed to. Yet how long had it been since he went to confession and Communion?

28

He was supposed to go to the Sacraments at least once a year. He wasn't a Catholic at all, really.

He was very humble when he left the house.

"God give you strength," his mother said, watching him go.

He did not answer her. He did not look at her.

He had not yet begun to change the world — as saints change it, dead or alive. But he had begun to make great changes in himself.

# 4

SIR JOSEPH GLYNN, in his matter-of-fact way states that Matt went to confession before he took the pledge, and that afterward he returned home "and on Sunday morning attended the 5 a.m. Mass at St. Francis Xavier's church," and went to Communion.

An American reader, interested in Matt and his possible canonization, wanted to know more about this epochal change. But he could find no further details, in Sir Joseph or any other authority. However, the time came, when, kneeling in the Pro-Cathedral in Dublin, he was able to fill in for himself some of the spaces the biographers had left blank.

It was a Saturday evening in June. The air was chill, and an ill-natured sky was trying to make up its mind to drench the Irish with cold rain. It was about seven o'clock, and still light outside. But it was dark and gloomy inside, despite all the candles and electric lights.

This church is one of the grimmest in Europe, one of the most bleak, and perhaps the most drafty. It is a big bare structure containing a lot of altars, and a lot of fat, round, tall, dark pillars that shut out most of the altars from one's vision. Its floor is stone, cold and relentless. Its wooden pews are old fashioned, uncomfortable, and ungracious. Its doors keep opening and closing constantly, letting in people or letting them out, and giving the drafts a chance to rush madly everywhere.

There are many confessionals, and on this evening there were long lines of men and women stretching toward each of them. Most of the people were on their knees. They moved slowly, up a dark aisle, around a pillar, toward a narrow bench. They moved a few inches at a time, not more than the width of the penitent who had moved first.

There was a patience in these Irish men and women the visitor thought remarkable. They were so still! There was so little fidgeting among them! There was so much reverence in them!

As soon as one had inched his way to a place on the bench, he got up off his knees, rubbed the stiffness out of his joints, and sat down. Then he moved, again a small distance at a time, closer and closer to the confessional. When, at last, he had reached the end of the bench he knelt again, to wait on the stone floor until it was his turn to enter the box and tell his sins.

Everyone went into the confessional with a minimum of noise. Some disappeared into its darkness timidly, some furtively, some with evident eagerness and relief. Everyone emerged unconscious of the noise his feet might make; and most of them were smiling.

It was not in the Pro-Cathedral that Matt had gone to confession that day in 1884. He went to the chapel of Holy Cross College — where a relic of the True Cross was kept. But in any church or chapel in Ireland, a visitor will see much the same thing on a Saturday night — great lines of penitents moving with the slowness and inevitableness of glaciers toward the wide warm Sea of Mercy.

So far as the American visitor was concerned, Matt Talbot

was one of the men in the nearest line. He was the balding little man with the Rosary in his left hand.

He had been years away from confession, and hours away from his last drink. He couldn't pray. He couldn't keep his mind on anything. He couldn't quite understand how he had come to be here. He should be in the pub. He needed a drink. At no time in his whole life had he needed one so much.

He could get it now. The fellows would be generous by this time. They would be eager to make up for their stinginess, their coolness. What was he doing here? Why did he stay in line? Why didn't he jump up and run out? It was crazy to think such a proper bowsie as Matt Talbot could keep the pledge for three whole months.

The people near him, men in overalls and in uniforms, men on their way home, men who hadn't had their suppers yet, and women — how many women there were — were they all here to take the pledge with him? Yes, but it would be a pledge not to lie, not to cheat, not to gossip, not to use profane language, not to commit any of the other sins they were used to committing.

That woman lighting a penny candle under the feet of the crucifix now — that was Matt's mother, the visitor pretended, praying for Matt and the rest of her brood. Her thin, haggard face was beautiful in the soft light of the candles. She touched the wick to a flame and put the candle in a little glass, and pushed the glass, shyly, a little closer to the holy feet than it had been before. That way, somehow, it resembled the lamp a mother places in the window, so that her children will find the way home without too much trouble.

She was a tired woman. Perhaps she had worked hard all day, and must go home, after confession, to scrub the floors and make everything neat and tidy for the Lord's day.

The priests in the confessionals, it occurred to the visitor, were like mothers. They too must make many rooms clean and tidy for the Lord's day. For the King of kings would go into each of those rooms on the morrow. Yes, they were mothers, in a sense. And even if the rooms came to them, one by one, and saved them the trouble of walking about, they were probably more tired at the end of the day than the average mother was.

The little man with the bald spot, the visitor noted, had reached the bench. He was sitting down, staring at the old woman who still stood beneath the crucifix. He was staring at her, but he didn't see her, evidently. He was absorbed.

Then, without warning, a priest was standing in the pulpit, somewhere behind one of those dark pillars, and he had started the Rosary in a loud voice — a loud voice with a soft Cork accent.

All the middle doors of the confessionals banged open. All the priests barged out. And each went hurrying his separate way from the church.

If someone had told the American that the priests had that moment gone on strike, he might have believed it. If all the penitents waiting to go to those priests to be relieved of their sins had got up off their knees, or off the benches where they sat, he would not have been surprised.

But the people in the aisles and on the benches did not move. The expression on the face of the little balding man did not alter in any way. The only change in him was that he had broken off his own Rosary to join in that of the priest in the pulpit.

A woman kneeling next to the visitor whispered an explanation.

"The poor priests," she said. "Ah, it's them that's worked to death every Saturday, and every holyday eve. In those dark little boxes, mind ye, since twelve or one o'clock, every man of them. Without letup. Without a bite or a sip all day long. Listening to all the sins of the world."

The visitor looked at his watch. It was a few minutes after eight o'clock.

"Now," the woman went on, "they'll be wolfing down a few cold victuals. A cold potato and an onion maybe. Then it's back they'll be hurrying to the job of cleansing us poor sinners. Lord, have mercy on them! Who wants to be a priest?"

Time had finished five decades of a Rosary of years since

33

Matt Talbot went to confession, that night in the eighties and took the pledge. And it was well into the second five decades. Yet what was time to the holy servant of God — or to the man from America? This may not have been the night nor the place Matt Talbot chose to repent of his drunkenness and to begin his life anew, but the conditions, the visitor felt, were the same.

He knew, somehow, as he walked up O'Connell Street toward his hotel, that the balding little man he had picked to represent Matt Talbot would be still sitting on the bench when the tide changed, and the priests came hurrying back to their confessionals. The man would still be tempted to get up and run. He would still be tormented by thirst, and by doubts of his ability to keep any pledge. He would still be unable to pray, or to fix his mind on anything except the awfulness of his plight and the terrible need he felt for the help of God and man.

The visitor felt he knew Matt Talbot a little better than before.

He tried to imagine how Matt's mother felt, greeting him when he returned home. But he couldn't. He kept thinking of the face of that woman who had placed the penny candle at the Saviour's feet.

He tried to imagine how Matt felt, going to Communion at that early Mass on Sunday morning. He couldn't. He tried to identify himself with Matt as he returned to the job on Monday morning. It was impossible.

Matt probably didn't hold any grudge against his tightwad pals. He liked them. He liked almost everybody. He must have figured they had done him a favor, driving him back to the Church. He was indebted to them. He would do a favor for them some day. He would pray for them. He would not tell them about the pledge. Matt was never one for talking about himself. Only rarely did he confide in anybody.

He would forgive them. But he would also avoid them, especially after working hours. Else he certainly would not keep his word to God.

All day Sunday he must have spent in getting ready for the return to the job, the return to the world. He must have outlined a plan of action. He must have determined to adopt some sort of routine to protect him from himself, and from his friends.

He would go to Mass every morning, he must have decided, before he went to work. Then, immediately after work, he would hurry away. He would go into the nearest church and stay there as long as he could. Thus he could be sure none of his friends would find him. Maybe, in time, he could learn to pray again. Only prayer could really help him.

"It's no use," he told his mother over and over again. "I can't possibly stay sober three months. Not with all the churches in Dublin."

It was no use, he was sure. But he would go down fighting.

Monday was a day of pure agony. Matt got out of bed while it was still dark, dressed hurriedly, and walked to the Jesuit church for 5 o'clock Mass. He was too early. The doors were not yet open. Should he wait?

Hadn't he waited for the pub to open so he could turn a little sawdust into a little ale for his aching body?

He knelt on the stone steps and waited.

This was the first of many vigils in the darkness and the cold, spent kneeling outside some Catholic church until the doors were opened.

Matt went to the Communion rail that morning as though he were in a race, and knelt at the extreme right of the altar. He didn't know how long it would take the priest to finish Mass, and he wasn't taking any chances. He had to be at work at 6 o'clock. He would walk out right after Communion. That would give him time to stop at his home and get breakfast before going on to work. Some priests were slow saying Mass. Some were fast. Sometimes there were many people at the altar rail, even at the early Masses. In any event, Matt must receive Communion before anybody else, so he could hurry away immediately. He had no watch, but he was a good judge of the passage of time.

It became the rule of his life thereafter to receive Communion as soon as possible in the morning, before anybody else in the congregation. But he usually stayed in the church until the priest had left the sanctuary.

A pick-me-up? With all the reverence of his heart, that's how Matt regarded early Mass and Communion. The Body and Blood, the Soul, and the Divinity of Christ! Meat indeed! Drink indeed! Courage, sustenance, aid, strength, life itself! A pick-me-up, a bracer, an inspiration to persevere, and even an interior coat of armor to protect him from all temptations!

He didn't feel that way in the beginning. There was no particular feeling in his first visits to the church, at least there was no feeling of devotion. He did know the wild thirst for drink, and the fear of succumbing to it. It is probable that he was still too numb for any special prayers. It is probable that the only prayer that reached the throne was the one recited by the panic of his heart: "God, don't let me go back to the booze."

Monday, Tuesday, Wednesday, Thursday, Friday, and Saturday of that first week it was the same. The sudden awakening. The awful awareness that something strange had happened, something that must be frightfully wrong. The slow understanding of the fact that he was sober — cruelly sober. The panic in wondering how long he would remain sober. The memory of the need for Mass and Communion. The quick preparation. The walk to the church. The waiting, outside, in the darkness and the chill. The rush to the Communion rail. The quick breakfast. The swift walk to work. The queer looks of the men around him.

The first crisis held off until Saturday noon. That was payday. Matt had eighteen shillings or so — or would have when the right barmaid cashed his check.

Now he was a different person than he had been the previous Saturday when he had nothing but a hang-over and a raging thirst. Now he was a popular fellow with all his mates.

"Good day, Matt," one said to him, " 'tis the long hard

drought is on me, and the longing for an elbow working next
to mine. Will ye have a pint with me, lad?"

"Sure there's yourself now," said another, "looking like
you could down a glass without any trouble at all, at all. And
me wondering all the week had ye broken your good right
arm or no, and getting an eyestrain from watching the door of
the pub for the sight of you coming in. Will ye h'ist a glass
with me, Matt?"

Matt thanked them, courteously, but gruffly. And he could
be quite gruff. He went into the pub with them, and got the
silver pieces his bit of paper entitled him to. But he did not
shove them back to the barmaid. He bought a bottle of mineral
water, and put the change where it belonged.

It was the last time he ever went into a pub, even to cash
a check. A man didn't have to be a slave, he had learned, even
to the petit larceny rules made by his bosses. If he were a
good workman, he could always threaten to quit and get a
better job.

Most of Matt's companions thought he was clowning with
that bottle of mineral water. They watched, in a state of
shock, as he drank it and put it back on the bar. Those closest
might have noticed that his hand was trembling as it put the
bottle down. But they were too dazed to notice anything except
that the proper bowsie was no longer one of them.

Matt walked slowly away from the place, sweating with the
effort to keep from turning around and hurrying back. He
quickened his pace. He saw a church. He scurried into its
darkness, its coolness, its peace, its protection. He stayed there
all afternoon.

"Arra, Mother," he said when he arrived home, "it's a
weakling I am. And worse. The thirst still burns in me like a
peat fire in a Donegal shanty. I'm fair crazy with the smoke of
it, and the heat of it, and the bitter taste of it. Sure I'll never
last three months."

"You will," his mother contradicted him. "With the help of
God you'll last three months; and longer. Sit down to your
dinner now, and you'll feel better before your dad says grace."

**37**

# 5

THE first time Matt came home drunk his father thrashed him. Matt got drunk again the next day. His father beat him again. And Matt got drunk again.

Charles Talbot felt that if he got Matt another job the boy might become a decent sort of man. He drank only because there was so much porter and ale and stout and wine there where he worked, Charles Talbot thought. A boy that young wouldn't have got the habit of drinking. Not yet. A new job would give him a new life. So, as soon as he could arrange it, Talbot managed to put his son to work for the Port and Docks board, as a messenger boy.

How the devil must have laughed!

There were stores of bonded whisky on the docks where young Matt was put for sobriety and safety. They were in the keeping of Matt's father, an honest and a sober man, a good man, a man who went to confession and Communion at least once a month, a man handing down a tradition. His father and his grandfather, you remember, had also kept these stores

38

and had kept them honestly and well. Someday, he hoped, when Matt had come to his senses, he too would be a foreman of the Port and Docks board, and an honest keeper of these supplies.

With what gusto the devil must have laughed!

It was made easy for the foreman's son to acquire all the whisky his growing thirst desired. He could have bottles not only for himself; he could also entertain his friends — in secret.

Eventually Matt saw what he was doing to his father. So he made a change. He did not give up drinking. The thought of doing such a foolish thing did not occur to him. He gave up his job, and got another, as a bricklayer's helper in the employ of a building contractor. He still had to depend on his father for food and clothing and a comfortable bed and all the other necessities of life, except hard liquor. He could buy his own now, and drink it where he pleased.

After he returned to sobriety, after he had begun to spend part of his evenings with his parents and his sisters, after he had begun again to say the Rosary with them before he went to bed, he wondered what he could do to repay them for all their patience, all their prayers.

His mother and father were members of the Confraternity of the Immaculate Conception, attached to St. Francis Xavier's Church. Matt joined them in this organization. And it was sometime after this that he began to make up for the dissipated years.

For weeks he still went about Dublin like a lost child, stumbling into churches to pray without words, coming home to sit for hours without speaking, and to kneel for family prayers without any hope, or any charity, or any faith. For weeks he kept telling his mother he would never stay sober three whole months. And for weeks a miracle of grace worked in him, a grace bestowed by the Lady of the Confraternity, the Lady of the Beads, the Mediatrix of All Graces.

Matt didn't realize how important it was, not only to himself and his family — and perhaps to thousands and thousands of others — but also to Our Lady of Grace, and to her Father,

Spouse, and Son, that he should stay sober and sanctify himself.

Few other men know the importance of this, have known it, or will ever know it. Few men know they are at all important, especially to God.

Some may recall the message of St. Peter to be sober and watch, because "your adversary, the devil, goeth about like a roaring lion seeking whom he may devour." But they attach little significance to these words, believing them a mere figure of speech. How can the devil be a roaring lion, some foolish ones insist, when he is a hissing serpent, or a sinister-looking man with concealed horns, cloven hoofs, and a tail? They do not know he can disguise himself in many ways. Few men know that, through strong drink, the devil seeks continually to devour men — and at the same time show his hatred and contempt of God!

Long before God made the world and the people in it, He gave the angels a vision of men. He permitted them to see His own Son take flesh in the womb of a virgin. He allowed them to see that Son giving His Body to men, in the appearance of bread and wine, in order that they might have eternal life.

The angels gazed on this incomprehensible and holy mystery; some with awe, and some with anger. Millions cried out, with Lucifer, their radiant leader, that they would not serve God if He should be made man. Forthwith these were pitched headlong by the Archangel Michael and his legions into the frozen fires of an everlasting hell. And, ever since, in their hatred they have made implacable and despairing war on God and men.

Ever since the first grapevines struggled up out of the darkness and cut through the crust of the earth God made for them, Lucifer and his legions have detested wine, and all the drinks that could be likened to it. Ever since the first field of grain waved in the winds of God, the hordes of hell have hated bread, and all the foods that could be encompassed in its name. Ever since the first man looked at the world and saw that it was good, and that God was good, the devil and all his imps have hated him.

Bread and wine were symbols of the first casting-out of devils. They were also the symbols of the Body, Blood, Soul, and Divinity of Jesus Christ. They were food and drink that, properly consecrated, would let the creature partake of the nature of the Creator!

From the very beginning Lucifer planned to destroy all men, to spite the God who loved and created them, and to keep them from filling the thrones in heaven left vacant by the rebel angels. God wanted them to partake of His Divinity? Lucifer would make them degraded and sodden beasts. And he would do it with the sacred symbols of bread and wine. A jibe at the omnipotence of God, and, at the same time, a slaughter of the innocents!

From the earliest ages the devil kept a tight grip on the world through bread and wine. Give the average man enough wine — or any other drink God would recognize as an instrument of the devil's mockery — and it was easy to debauch and enslave him. Wine, under the right conditions, could foment the ghastliest massacres, the bloodiest wars, the coldest treacheries, the most obscene blasphemies, the awfulest human woes.

Man might be a speck of dust destined to shine in immortal glory; but sufficient drink would turn him into mud, to fill a hole in the pitted paths of hell.

Give a man too much wine and you could take bread away from his wife and children. Get the men first. Women and children would follow.

Women must be given especial attention by the devil, for one of them would rise up someday — if God had His way — to crush him. They would try to save their men, at first. They would visit the altars of their silly gods, or fly into the church of the One True Deity, and prostrate themselves in prayer. But they might get tired, after a time, and argue that "sauce for the gander was sauce for the goose." The devil could be patient — for his own ends.

The children might pray too, pitifully. But how many children of drunkards know anything about prayer?

**41**

Christ, when He arrived, would say to a woman of Canaan, "It is not good to take the bread of the children, and to cast it to the dogs." He would tell His Apostles to suffer the little children to come unto Him, for "of such is the kingdom of heaven."

Lucifer intended that the drunken father should throw the children's bread to worse than the dogs; and he intended the little children to come to him, not to Christ. To this end he provided destitution, hunger, shame, squalor, disease, ignorance, and other little gifts. He provided these with the help of the children's parents — those who poured the stinking city slums out of their steins or mugs or horns or glasses.

Matt Talbot, as tightly chained to the devil of drink as any other slave, stepped suddenly out of line. He was not the first. He will not be the last. But the devil knew that, in the course of time, he would rescue many others from that line. He didn't like Matt Talbot. He tried to get him back, by the ordinary methods used in such cases. He failed.

Pity the devil. (Pity him and you hurt him badly. He cannot endure pity or ridicule. He cannot stand any sort of kindness. He shrivels under such treatment, and hurries away.) Pity the eternal schizophrenic, the immortal split personality who can never forget either heaven or hell, and who is continually, despite his victories, frustrated and outmaneuvered and set back by almighty God.

Matt tried to keep away from him, sojourning in a land he did not know was Egypt — where Christ and Joseph and Mary waited in exile for the death of Herod. Lucifer followed him into this Nile valley of the churches, into the sanctity of his father's home. Matt could not get rid of the pest, because he had not yet won back the grace of prayer. Neither could he fight his enemy, for our Lady had not yet let him learn what power there was in Bread and Wine.

It is possible too, that, like many other Christians, Matt had then no belief in the actuality of Satan. So many people think his sulphuric majesty is as fictional as Santa Claus! The devil planned it that way. He wants the world to think there

42

is no hell, hence no devil. That makes it easier for him to operate.

If Matt was a disbeliever in Satan, or Lucifer, or the powers of darkness in general, he was quickly and rudely set aright. The demon confronted him one morning in front of the Jesuit church, and showed his displeasure to Matt in a manner any man could understand.

Matt was walking into the church, after waiting outside on his knees. He was half awake and half asleep, for it was early, and he hadn't slept well. He was thinking that he needed a drink. He was thinking also that he needed Mass and Communion even more.

Without warning he was violently pushed back and to one side. He looked around him, but could see no one. Was he drunk, then, and imagining things? He didn't think so. He went forward the second time, perturbed if not exactly frightened, and now wide awake. Something pushed him back again, more roughly than before.

Matt couldn't think of anything but the devil. The fury of hell was trying to keep the poor little man out of the church, trying to shunt him off to the nearest pub, trying to make him break the pledge and return to his collar and chains.

Matt could get just as rough as any bouncer from hell, he thought. And perhaps he remembered that the Irishman does not run from an enemy but at him. He charged, this time, using the names of Jesus and Mary as bayonet jabs, and sent the devil downstairs where he belonged.

It may have been in the evening of that same day that Matt's sister Mary brought home a present for him, to celebrate his release from alcohol. Matt was not home. He did not arrive until quite late. Mary thought she knew the reason.

"We'll say the Rosary without him," she said.

Her mother sighed.

"Yes," she said. "We'll say it without him; and we'll say it for him."

"I brought him a book," Mary said. "Little he cares, and

him breaking his pledge almost as soon as he took it." She threw the book furiously into a dark corner. "The devil fly away with it," she said.

Then Matt came in, sober, but harassed and weary.

He shook his head at the two women, as though to say it was no use, no use at all to keep on fighting; he would not stay sober another day. The pull of the liquor was too strong in him.

Mary retrieved the book from the corner, undid its wrapping, and handed it to her brother.

"It's for you," she said, shy suddenly, and vexed with herself for many reasons. "It's to — to help you."

Matt looked at it stupidly. A book! Of all things in the world! She wanted him to read a book! Sure, that way madness lay. What had got into the lass at all, at all? Didn't she know he had never read a book, that he never would?

He looked at the title, spelling out the letters slowly to himself. *Hell Open to Christians.*

Glory be to God, what a thing for a sister to give a brother trying to crawl out of a hell of his own!

He turned a few pages, looked at the crude pictures of sinners being tormented by imps, and shut the book. It "frightened the life out of him," he later confided to his mother. But he did not want either of the women to know that then.

" 'Tis decent of you, Mary," he said. "And maybe I need it more than you know."

He found time to read it many times before he died. It was in his room, with other well-read books, the morning he dropped dead. It had lost its original covers. Matt had rebound it.

If Matt had had any doubts about the reality of the devil after his encounter outside the doors of the Jesuit church, and after reading his sister's gift book, those doubts vanished for all the rest of his life as a result of his next encounter.

This occurred some years after he had got into the habit of going to Mass and Communion every morning, and of attending all the Masses on Sundays. Nobody is sure of the date. Matt was not sure of it himself. It was "within two or three years" after he took the pledge, he said.

He was in St. Francis Xavier's Church. It was a Sunday morning. During the early Mass he got up and started toward the altar rail. He stood still, unable to take a step forward. He felt something filling his soul as with absolute despair. He was certain he could not go on fooling himself or God any longer. He was convinced he would get drunk again, tomorrow if not today, that he would leave the Church again, that he would be damned.

He tried to move ahead, but he was powerless. He tried to think clearly. But there was nothing in his mind except the awful need of drink — he must have a drink immediately — and the hopelessness of his plight. He turned and walked out of the church. He wandered through the streets of Dublin, as he had wandered in the days of his alcoholic haze. He didn't know where he was going nor why.

About 8 o'clock he saw that he was in front of the Pro-Cathedral. He went in and knelt before the main altar. He felt well. He got up to go to Communion, and the temptation numbed and confused him again, and drove him back into the streets. At 9 o'clock, or thereabouts, the same thing happened in another church.

Shortly before the 10 o'clock Mass began in St. Francis Xavier's, Matt found himself back there, on the steps outside the gates. He threw himself down, stretched out his arms to make a cross of his body, and moaned in anguish, heedless of all those near him, who could not help but think he was disgracefully befuddled.

He lay there abjectly, no one speaking to him, no one bending over him to see if he were sick or dying or just drunk. And he prayed. He prayed aloud. He prayed to our Lady and to her Son. He prayed to be delivered from the tempter and from all temptation.

"Please," he implored, "don't let me go back to my old ways. God, have mercy on me. Mary, help me."

Yes, it is quite possible that Matt spent many hours in

45

prayer for those who needed help, even as he needed it in that hour. It is quite possible he still intercedes for them, and that he always will while time runs on.

After a few minutes of prayer the burden of despair was lifted from him. He rose, joyously, walked sedately into the church, wedged himself into his favorite niche, and waited for Communion as confidently as any banker. This time nothing stopped him when he went to the altar.

Matt may have encountered the evil one again in his later years, for God permits the eternal frustrate to tempt His holy servants — perhaps that the servants may attain glory, and the tempter new frustrations. If so, there is no record of it.

# 6

THE reformed drinkers who make up the membership of Alcoholics Anonymous, are controlled — and blessed — by a great fear, a terror akin to the fear of the Lord, for it is the beginning of wisdom. It is the fear of taking the first drink after they have been "cured." All that stands between them and grave disaster, they know, is that one drink.

Matt Talbot was ruled — and blessed — by this same fear. And for him it was indeed the beginning of wisdom.

He realized, in the torment of his thirst, that he must be stronger than his thirst if he were to remain sober. He realized he must be stronger than his body. In order to be stronger than his body he must strengthen his will at the expense of his body. He must make himself master of his body — and he could do that only in a way recommended by many saints. He could do it by fasting and penance, only through fasting and penance.

Thus, shortly after he took the pledge, and about the time he had his first physical fight with Old Noxious, he began to practice austerities that have led some ecclesiastic writers to class him among the "great penitents," and still others to rank him with the "great contemplatives."

Father Edmund, C.P., in a foreword to Rev. Jas. F. Cassidy's book, *Matt Talbot, the Irish Workers' Glory*, makes this flat statement:

> For Matt Talbot was a contemplative, one whose soul continually turned towards God, one whose mind was absorbed in God. The magnitude of this achievement has not, we think, been sufficiently recognized. By far the great majority of contemplatives, whether canonized or not, have been members of religious orders. Their lives were sheltered by the walls of monastery or convent, the distractions of the world were reduced to a minimum or eliminated altogether; they were helped by the good example of companions, and were assisted by assiduous direction and frequent spiritual conferences. Not so with Matt Talbot. For a cloister he had the busy streets of his native city; for a cell the back room of a tenement house, for companions men who had little appreciation of spiritual realities; for a place of retirement a shed in the corner of the timber-yard. Yet to such a place did the Spirit of God descend to take him by the hand and to lead him up the steep places to the mystic mount of prayer.

And Father Cassidy cannot help speaking of the "golden days of Ireland's early monastic church" when he begins to talk of Matt.

> Though only a humble laborer [he says] far removed from the influence of conventual discipline, the record of his austerities bears comparison with the best of saintly anchorite or monk of old. Perhaps we could go further and say that, considering the circumstances of his life, it eclipses, in all likelihood, most penitential records of the past. While the disciplinary severities of the anchorites were part and parcel of the life they professed, Talbot's not only came into being despite the character of his vocation, but transformed him into a hermit in the midst of the world. The cross on which he chose to immolate himself could not be the cross he desired, were it not hidden from the eyes of men; and this cross of

48

concealment kept him in severe spiritual isolation from the world.

Matt, fittingly enough, began his new life by pinning the sign of the cross on his coat sleeve. He used two pins; and he put them where he could see them most frequently. He would have stared with suspicion and anger at anybody who suggested he was taking up the cross in the manner of the old crusaders. If he knew what a crusader was, he never would have included himself in their ranks.

Those two pins were to remind him, every so often, to make an act of contrition, if only in his mind, for all the times he had used the name of God in vain, for all the times he had listened to the filthy stories of his drinking companions, and for all the other sins of commission or omission of which he had been guilty.

They were also to remind him that Christ had suffered and died on a cross for him, and that he now had the privilege of suffering for Christ. He could suffer in atonement for his sins. He could suffer in reparation for the sins of others. He could grow strong through suffering. And the more generous he was in inflicting sufferings on himself the more generous heaven would be in giving him the graces he needed.

One grace he wanted especially, if he was to persevere. That was the grace of prayer. It was odd, but it was true, that one must pray for the grace of prayer, and pray for it earnestly, devoutly, and constantly.

A glance at the crossed pins sticking into the shoddy cuff of his overcoat sleeve was an invitation to prayer, a meditation, a memento, an inspiration, a stimulant more powerful than any ever bottled.

It wasn't enough, naturally, to make himself a knight of the two pins. He began to deprive himself of one or two meals a day. His mother was grieved at this, thinking perhaps her cooking was to blame. But when he refused meat on all Wednesdays, Fridays, and Saturdays, she began to understand.

His body could rail at him now with serious complaints.

"First you take away my liquor; now you take away my meat. Soon you'll have me on less than beggar's rations. Wurra wurra, how long do you think you can keep me in this state?"

But Matt wasn't listening to complaints. He was making them.

"You're too easy on yourself," he said. "Look at the nice pipe you bought yourself the other day. Just because you had money in your pocket. Sure you might have sent that silver to some missionary in China or Africa or America, instead of filling it with the ashes of the money you wasted on tobacco. You'll give the pipe away this day. Aye, and the tobacco also. And you'll do without tobacco from now on. That'll teach you, me bucko. You'll get no sympathy from me."

"But I'm a workingman," the body argued. "I work hard. Be reasonable, Matt. Is it trying to starve me entirely you are? Is it that afraid you are of going back to the liquor, and that mean about it that you have to punish me — like the man who beats his wife because he's mad at the foreman?"

"Punish, is it?" one can hear Matt answering. "Man, you don't know what punishment is yet. I'll let you have a decent meal on Sunday. Sometimes, maybe, two meals. But it's dry bread and tea on Monday and Tuesday and Thursday, and maybe a trifle of meat with it now and then. Black tea at that, without sugar. Fridays — that's the day you'll catch it now — Fridays will be full fast days for the likes of you. And wait until I get you into Lent."

"Lent!"

"And June," Matt would continue, ruthlessly, "the month of the Sacred Heart, that'll be another Lent to you, from now on. Maybe that'll teach you who's the boss."

Matt, after the first few weeks of his three months' novitiate as a reformed alcoholic, became so busy inflicting new penances and disciplines on himself, new ways of mastering his body and all its appetites, that he stopped telling his mother he could not continue to stay sober. When the three months had passed he took a pledge for a year. And he knew that he would keep it. At the end of the year he took the pledge for life.

Alcoholics Anonymous is a "mutual-help" organization. Everybody in it believes in helping every other alcoholic. Thus one seldom hears, nowadays, the old familiar adage that "there's no one so intolerant of drunks as an ex-drunk."

Matt Talbot, though, in the first days of recognizing himself as an ex-drunk, might have been tabbed among the most intolerant of reformers. While he was still reforming himself he attempted to reform his brothers. He told them what they looked like, coming home at all hours and waking everybody in the house as they stumbled toward their beds. He told them how they were affecting their parents. They reminded him he had not bothered about that for a great many years. He had, in fact, hurt his parents more by his drinking than had any one of them. Who else, they asked him, had ever been so crazy for booze that he would pawn his shoes for it and walk miles home in his socks?

He tried to compel them to reform. They wouldn't have it that way. He told them to get out of the house. They told him to take his own advice.

Eventually Matt rented himself a room in Gloucester Street, which wasn't far away from his parents' home, and made an arrangement with his sister Mary to look after the place, and to do whatever cooking he might require.

One day shortly after he had installed himself in the room, Mary saw two planks lying in a corner. That bothered her. Who, in his right mind, would bring such rough lumber into a bedroom? And what would he do with them, once they were there? They were heavy, rough, unplaned, nailed together. Surely Matt wasn't going to whittle them to while away the time in this lonely place?

"Arra, now, Matt," Mary said, "there's little enough room here as it is without cluttering up so much of it with those dirty planks. What in the name of all that's holy made you bring them here?"

"I had my reasons," Matt said easily. "They're for a purpose."

Mary tried — give her credit — but she could get no more

out of him than that. Yet she found out the purpose just the same. She discovered, one night when Matt had gone to a night service in the Jesuit church, that he had placed the planks on the rough iron bed in the corner and concealed them with a coverlet.

How Mary happened to make this discovery has not been written down. That is, biographers do not know whether she suspected Matt's objective, and waited outside until she saw him leave, so she could slip in and make sure; or whether, in a sisterly attempt to make a brother's bed look neater than it was, she accidentally found the wood.

It was probably in this room, and on those planks, that Matt first learned to kneel upright, without support, and to maintain a rigid attitude for hours.

Those who knew Matt best — people who went to church with him — say he remained kneeling all through Mass, except when he went to the Communion rail. He remained on his knees even during the Gospel. On Sunday, after the first Mass, he would stay, without moving, for six or seven hours, his eyes shut, his bare knees pressed into the wooden kneeler, his arms crossed, his elbows not resting on anything, his body from the knees up as rigid and straight as the candles burning in adoration on the altar.

He had slit his trousers lengthwise so that the kneelers would feel harder to his body than otherwise. And he wore a long thin overcoat, buttoned carefully to hide his naked knees from passers-by, when he went about the city.

He told a friend, some years before he died, that he had read, in a book he didn't name, that one could concentrate best in this manner, motionless, fixed, absorbed beyond all concession to fatigue or pain.

There was a boy in Italy, who died a few years before Matt even thought of reading books, who may have influenced him. This was Mickey Magone, "General Mickey," one of the boys about whom St. John Bosco wrote.

Mickey developed the habit of letting other boys go to confession before him. He would go toward Don Bosco's box

52

early in the evening, and kneel on the floor. But he wouldn't enter the box until everybody else had done so. Sometimes he remained thus, motionless, for hours.

Another boy who thought himself just as tough as Mickey, if not tougher, tried to imitate him. But he could not maintain the upright position for more than half an hour. He fainted.

It is possible Matt had read some pamphlet or tract about the young Italian — for he seems to have copied another trick of his with changes to suit his own personality.

Mickey was in his early teens when he died. He had a horror of profanity and dirty stories. Whenever he heard a friend abusing the sacred name, or telling an off-color yarn, he would steal quietly up behind the offender and whistle shrilly in his ear.

Matt was not one for whistling in anybody's ear; so he changed the procedure. He took off his hat, in reverence to the name he had heard so publicly dishonored. It was even more disconcerting, in time, than Mickey's boyish method.

The plank bed helped Matt in the fight to subjugate his body. He added a wooden pillow, to give his will all the best of it. After that the body had no chance. The odds were a thousand to one against it.

Who that makes his bed on a hard plank can fail to imagine how Christ felt, lying on the cross, with the nails holding fast His hands and His feet, the ropes binding His arms to the wood, and the thorns digging deeper into His head with every movement of His body?

Who that uses a block of wood for a pillow can help thinking of the agony of the crown of thorns? Who can help feeling that Pilate's sign is just above his bleeding head — "Jesus of Nazareth, King of the Jews!" Who can fail to hear the plaintive noise it makes in the wind? The sound of its rustling can be detected in spite of the furious cries and the laughing jeers of the mob, the sobs of Mary Magdalen, and the rattle of the soldiers' dice.

"Jesus of Nazareth, King of the Jews!" A man lying on a plank bed, resting his head on a heavy chunk of wood, can

53

read the sign in the dark. He can almost reach up an arm and pull it down to kiss it. A man lying still, or kneeling upright, can almost see the blood of Jesus leaping up from the nail holes as though glad to be freed of its Divine Prison so that it might free all prisoners of the devil.

A man dropping off to sleep, stretched out on the bare wood, can often feel himself quite close to all the power he needs, for himself, for his kindred, for his friends, and for all the other sinners in the world.

A man waking on a cross of his own devising must regard it as only a minor thing to remain, absorbed in contemplation, for a few hours, on his knees.

# 7

WHEN Matt was eighteen or nineteen his mother began to pray that he would meet some good girl, fall in love with her, and marry her. The right girl would make him stop drinking, she believed. The right girl would make a wonderful man of him. (But then, of course, the lass needn't be praising herself too highly, for she had good material to work with.)

Matt only laughed whenever she mentioned the subject. And the silly gossoon never looked twice at any of the colleens she or her daughters brought into the house.

"There you go again," he would say. "Is it getting rid of me you would be? And you my own mother? Arra now, don't you know it's only yourself I want? Or are you trying to make me tell you again that you are all the women I want?"

Mrs. Talbot's hopes for her favorite son rose high when he quit drinking. Surely he would get married now. He would need somebody to help him fight. He would need a woman who loved him, a good, steady, sensible body who knew how to cook and sew and mend, and do the wash herself, and keep

55

the house clean, and the babies healthy, and himself happy.

But Matt still felt the same foolish way about it. There'd be no grandchildren from that one, drunk or sober.

The idea became a certainty when she learned of Matt's curious romance.

Matt was in his early thirties then, and still in the employ of the building contractor. He was one of a gang chosen to work on the home of an Anglican minister. The girl worked in that house. She was the minister's cook.

She liked Matt from the first sight of him, although she had to admit he was an odd little man. She liked the way he took off his rusty iron bowler when the Angelus rang at noon, and the reverent way he stood, saying the words aloud, even if the minister himself was close enough to listen or not.

She liked the nice ways of him with the maids in the house, the soft words he spoke to them — "yes, Miss," or "no, Miss," or "if you please, Miss," or "if it be no trouble to you, Miss." Ah, and the downcast eyes of him; and the sweetness of his smile! It wasn't really a smile; it just seemed to be a smile. His face lighted up for a moment, and something wonderful happened to his eyes. And then it was gone. Faster than lightning it came and went.

There was mystery in that, mystery enough for any woman.

And there were other things a woman wouldn't be knowing anything about, many other things, in that fleeting smile the little man let one see occasionally.

She liked his quick, competent, happy handling of the bricks, his sureness of movement, his serenity under all conditions, and his looking up to heaven now and then, when there was a pause in the work and nobody was talking to him. He looked at the sky in the way a man looks at a field on which he has a mortgage, or which he intends to buy.

And, once in a while, if you kept your eyes on him, you might see him fingering a Rosary when he had nothing special to attend to; hiding the beads in one of his big rough hands when anybody ventured close to him.

Perhaps, too, the cook was sorry for Matt. A scrawny man

he was for all the strength he showed. Sure, a self-respecting cannibal wouldn't eat him, even parboiled before roasting. What sort of mother was it that stood by and let his bones stick out that way, crying for the fat a decent cook could give them?

Matt hardly said hello to her, and when he did he was looking at the ground between his feet, and she knew he couldn't tell whether she was blonde or redheaded or jet black, let alone give anyone the color of her two big lonesome eyes. So she had to talk to him.

And he would not propose to her. So she had to propose to him.

" 'Tis not as if either of us was still too young to be making up our minds," she explained. "I speak for myself at any rate. I know what I'm saying, Matt. I know what I want. And don't be telling me you are but a workingman, and poor as our Lord Himself. I've enough put by for both of us. Our own home we can have. And decent meals for you every day in the week, and the grand fine meal on Sunday. 'Tis not a bad cook I am, Matt Talbot, if it's myself that has to say so. Come in now, and sit down for a minute while you're waiting on the lorries, and I'll feed you a bit of my stew."

How Matt felt about it we don't know. The story comes from Matt's mother, and, secondhandedly, through her daughter Mary.

All we know is that Matt told the girl he would make a novena to our Lady, and ask what was her will, and the will of God. And we know that, after the novena, he told the girl that marriage was not for him; and that years later Matt told a trusted friend — possibly Raphael O'Callaghan — that the Blessed Virgin had told him not to marry.

Mrs. Talbot never again suggested marriage to her son Matt, nor did she mention any woman's name to him. She had learned, at last, the name of the woman he loved, and the immeasurable measure of his love for her.

That woman, she realized now, with joy, had taken care of Matt all his days, in his childhood when he ran away from school, and in his adolescence and early manhood when he ran away from God. It was she who had brought him back to God, her Son. It was she he loved; and he loved her as maid and mother, as sister and guide and tender protector, as the queen of saints and angels, and as the queen of women.

Matt came home after his brothers had left the house, bringing his books and furniture with him; and he lived there until after the death of his father, in 1899.

We have a better idea of Charles Talbot than we have of Matt. He looked, many people have said, "exactly like the picture of the father of St. Therese, the Little Flower." The circumstances of his death have not been given to us, but he must have died happy, convinced that one of his twelve children, if not all of them, was a tremendous saint.

Mrs. Talbot, after the funeral, went to live with Matt in the drab place in Upper Rutland Street. Wasn't it the grand life she lived, with the Rosary always in one hand or the other — like a young girl with her first love letter, and she unwilling to set it down anywhere lest something happen to it — and the nights always so full of prayer and mystery and splendor? Wisha, sometimes she didn't feel like a widow at all.

Ah, it was grand indeed. But it was weird too, and exciting at times beyond all the telling of it. And, at other times, the choke in the throat for the very wonder of it all.

Sure there were moments when a woman couldn't help but think there was a daughter-in-law in the flat as well as herself and her son. A daughter-in-law, God save the word! Sure, no other woman ever had such a one, unless it might be St. Monica — she that was mother to St. Augustine and knew how thoroughly he was wedded to the Virgin Mother!

Oh, but it was exciting to be a Catholic, and to realize how closely we are related to all the souls in heaven, and to the Father, Son, and Holy Ghost that created, redeemed, and sanctified us. It was exciting, and it was puzzling, and awesome — and almost frightening, at times, in the intensity of the feelings it engendered.

Mrs. Talbot would wake in the dark, some nights, she told

her daughters, and listen to her son talking to the Queen of heaven.

He would be kneeling on the floor or on the planks of his bed. And he would hold long conversations with the Mystical Rose, talking to her with sweet words, and listening for her answer with his face so serious, so joyous, so rapt, or so sad!

Now and then he would throw himself headlong at the Lady's feet, and stretch out his arms to right and left, making a cross of his body. He would fall to the floor as though the weight of his love had been too heavy to bear and had flattened him out, or as though he wished to prove he was her slave, her humble, eager, devoted, and most loving slave.

Matt left his work in the brickyards, sometime in 1892, when the Jesuits decided to change the hour of the first Mass from 5 o'clock to 6:15. He had to be at work by 6. There might be other churches where he could hear an early Mass and still get to work on time; but they were far away. It did not occur to him that he might go to work without going to Mass at all.

He found a job in the lumberyards of T. and C. Martin, just across the Liffey River, which started at 8 o'clock. That gave him ample time not only to attend the early Mass, but also to make the Stations of the Cross before going to breakfast. He loved to make the Stations, and he has told friends he would crawl on his knees from station to station, except that it would attract attention to him.

He also had time to walk leisurely to work, and to stop at this church or that, visiting the Lord and Lady on his way.

And it was nice to work in the new place. Matt didn't say so, but his mother must have known how he felt in the lumberyards. Shoving timbers around, he must have melted into St. Joseph working in his carpenter shop, even into Jesus carrying the heavy beams St. Joseph needed in his work. Inhaling the smell of new wood, cut from trees in many parts of the world and brought to Dublin in great slow-moving boats, he must have felt himself as close to the Master — that other Workman — as he was when he settled himself at night on his planks and rested his head on the wooden pillow.

The work ended at 6 o'clock in the evening. Matt changed clothes, paid a visit to Christ and Mary in the church of St. Lawrence O'Toole, not far from the yards, and then walked leisurely home.

While she was able to do it, Mrs. Talbot got supper for him. It was ready when Matt came in. It wasn't ever much of a meal. A few vegetables, perhaps, a crust of bread, a pot of strong hot tea. (But not too strong, for tea was expensive, and if one bought too much of it one could not send so much to the missionaries.)

Matt kissed the crucifix, sometimes even before he kissed his mother. Then he knelt while he ate. And why not — since perhaps there were legions of angels there, and saints, and, for all anybody could say to the contrary, the Holy Family as well?

Afterward mother and son would say the Rosary together, and a few litanies, and other prayers. Some nights Matt would read to her out of books he had bought or borrowed. Some nights he would tell her stories about saints and angels. He had his pet saints, as every Catholic does.

He liked the penitents especially. St. Mary Magdalen and St. Mary of Egypt were among his favorites. He gave them as much praise and love and fatuous devotion as the American fan gives her current movie heroines. But his language was not extravagant when he discussed them. They were grand girls, he would tell somebody. And to another he would admit thinking them great girleens.

St. Michael, the archangel, was another intimate friend; and Matt seemed to be sorry, at times, that he hadn't known the heavenly warrior earlier. Suppose he had invoked him too, that day outside St. Francis Xavier's, when the scum of perdition was pushing him around! The names of Jesus and Mary had sufficed. They always suffice. But the addition of the name of Michael adds something to the devil's shame.

St. Therese, the "Little Flower," was almost like a daughter and a sister and a sweetheart to him. The other St. Teresa, the mystic, was likewise a great girl in Matt's estimation. And there were multitudes of others his mother had never heard of that he liked to talk about.

Some nights he would talk only about the Blessed Virgin. Some nights he would spend singing hymns.

But, praying, reading, telling stories, or lifting his voice in song, Matt remained on his knees.

At 10:30 o'clock, or perhaps a little earlier, he would go to bed with a statue of the Virgin and Child in his right arm. He was odd about that statue, his mother noticed. In the first place he had searched all over Dublin for the right one, and it had taken a long time to find it. The Infant rested on the Virgin's left arm; and the figures were so formed that they fit well against his body. Hence there was little difficulty that he would hurt them, turning in his sleep — though usually he didn't turn.

Also, it was so shaped that, hug it close to him as he might, it would not dig into his flesh and wake him.

In the second place, he hardly ever looked at the statue during the night — or if he did, he turned his eyes in some other direction lest his mother get to thinking silly things. He could be even gruff about it at times. But he wouldn't think of lying down without it. It was to him, at bedtime, more precious and more necessary than the most beautiful doll could be to the most passionate and loving of doll-crazy little girls.

It was essential that Matt go to sleep at once. (Perhaps he kissed the statue slyly, in the dark, before he closed his eyes. His mother wouldn't see that. She wouldn't know, did he kiss the Child and the Mother both, did he kiss either of them, or did he kiss the statue at all? But she had her own ideas.) Matt had to go to sleep immediately because he would wake up at 2 o'clock, to pray for two hours or more before venturing out to early Mass.

This was another mortification he forced upon his rebellious, drink-craving, and ever unruly body — the lack of sleep. For many years — no biographer can say just how many — he limited his sleep to three and a half hours.

Changing the hour of the early Mass didn't alter Matt's timetable in the slightest. Sometimes it was a little after 4 when he arrived in front of the Jesuit church. The doors wouldn't open until 6. But there was no law against a man's waiting peacefully on the steps until the time came. And if God sent the bitter wind through and through his starved, thin, ill-clad body, ah Glory be! wasn't that in the nature of a divine caress?

And what could a man offer God more dear to Him than His own caress, accepted and endorsed, unless it be to give Him His own Son? That gift he would give too. At the Mass. Let him give the lesser gifts first, the cold, the weariness, the pain in his knees, the denial of the rights that sleep had over him, the denial of all the other just claims of the flesh.

Let him give these little gifts, and let him love the wind that buffeted and stabbed him and rattled his very teeth — even as he loved the snow, and the rain, and the sleet, and the sunshine, and the moonlight, and the glitter of the stars, and the rocks and trees and flowers and insects and animals and immortal men and women God had created.

Let him curb his impatience for Brother Furlong to come along and open the House of God. He must wait a few hours to talk to God? Now that was too bad! But then, how many years had God waited, in sublime patience, to speak to the likes of a proper bowsie named Matt Talbot?

Matt would breakfast at home. His mother would have it ready. It was seldom more than a piece of dry bread and a sip of tea.

When he had gone to work Mrs. Talbot would clean up the room, make her son's bed and her own, then hurry off to Mass. She too was a daily Communicant, until the last few years of her life. Then the priest came once a month, bringing her the majesty, the divinity, the splendor, the holiness, the beauty, and the perfect joy of God, in the appearance of a white thin disk of unleavened bread — bringing God Himself.

# 8

THE hardest part of Matt's new job, hard as it was, was not the work itself. That was, at first, merely helping to unload the ships that came through all the seven seas into the Liffey and docked at the Martin wharf. Some of them would have great piles of lumber on their decks, the wood wet with spray and storm, and some of the boards caked with such gobs of salt it couldn't help getting under a man's nails. Even with the slings at work it was no easy task unloading cargo, piling the lumber neatly, or putting it into the waiting lorries.

The hard part of the job was the breaking-in of a new set of men to the acceptance of Matt's characteristics.

That business of the hat now. Everyone in the brickyards was well aware that Matt tipped his bowler in reverence whenever the holy name was uttered in his presence. Everyone there knew that he said the Angelus, especially at noon. And not a man jack of them minded.

It was different among the lumber and the waiting ships. The first time Matt said the Angelus there — it was at noon, and the bells of St. Lawrence O'Toole were ringing sweetly — the men stared in awe, and some broke into jeers.

Matt had been bending over a little pile of boards when he heard the first note of the bells. He straightened up. He jerked off his hat, and blessed himself, and shut his eyes and prayed. He heard the laughter and the words of ridicule.

He kept praying to the end. And then he looked at the rabble, scowling and silent, his hat in his hard fingers, his bald head shining in the sun. He was angry at the men, and he was sorry for them, and he was defiant of each and all of them. They left off laughing, for the time.

But there would be new ships in tomorrow, and new crews on them with the same ignorance and bigotry in their hearts, the same contempt and intolerance in their laughter.

And there would be men who cursed — decent men, perhaps, who thought it was the manly way of talking; and ignorant men who could express emotions only through strong language. There would be men who cursed more or less naturally, as a habit; and there would be those who cursed merely to plague the little man with the big black iron pot of a hat and make him keep lifting it all day, to see which should tire first, the blackguard tongue or the adoring arm.

Malachy Gerard Carroll, in his *Story of Matt Talbot*, likes to think of Matt "standing on the wharf, head bent, the chimes and the cry of the sea gulls around him, his figure one with the dust and the grime, and the oily waters." He likes to think of the picture as a symbol of "heat and sweat and dust and scummy water . . . a thing of beauty . . . lifted into the presence of the Holy Trinity."

Put old-fashioned schooners into the background, and some of the modern steamboats that came, with their iron hulls, out of the Civil War in America. Put piles of lumber here and there. And cumbrous old-fashioned wagons. And great strong horses with docked tails. And men of all kinds, sailors, dockers, teamsters, buyers and sellers, and those who just came down to the wharf because they had nowhere else to go. Then you will see Matt and his daytime world — a brave little man stopping in the middle of the day to show his love to Mary and his unconcern for all the opposition gathered around him.

He was a hard man to know, the others soon learned. He was rough, but, bedad, he was a kindly fellow too, if you were in trouble. He liked to be alone; but there was something about him, something distinguishing and unique, that gave him the right to be alone, and so prevented anybody from feeling offended when he walked off by himself to eat his noon lunch somewhere far from the chaffing and chattering mouths of his fellows.

No, he wasn't an easy man to get acquainted with; but then he was usually so silent and so inconspicuous that he was easy to forget. One would see him edging away from the gang at the noon hour to hide behind a pile of two-by-fours, and one might think he was going to say the beads in private before or after he ate. Matt was "a great one for religion," but, then, it wasn't a bad weakness — religion.

Sometimes the little fellow would step aside while the gang was waiting for the wagons to come up. But he was always there when the wagons must be loaded. Sometimes he left the creosote works for half an hour or more — but that was when the sleepers were cooking — the heavy logs that would lie in the roadbed of some railway after they had soaked in their pungent juices. Matt would use that time to attend a Mass in St. Lawrence O'Toole's, or maybe just to make a visit. It depended on the time of day and the length of time the railroad ties required. He hated to go into the church, though, with the smell of creosote or tar saturating his clothing. He was fastidious about many things, and especially about his appearance before the altar. He loved the beauty of the Lord's House, and the place where His glory dwelleth; and he felt he must be scrupulously clean in body and in soul — and even in his clothing — when he entered that House.

He asked to be put in the creosote yard only because he had to get away from the wharf with its unending profanity and tides of dirty stories. He asked, later, to leave the creosote yards. And, in due time, he found himself made "storekeeper," and shifted to a location known as Castle Forbes — probably because once there had been a shanty there owned by somebody named Kelly or O'Reilly or McCann.

A man can't get very far away from family traditions, Matt must have thought. His father and his grandfather and his great grandfather had all kept stores on the docks of Dublin. And Matt was as honest in his responsibility as any of his forebears, seeing to it that not even the least scraps of lumber were carried out of his domain without the proper written orders.

A sort of office went with the job, a few boards knocked together to make four walls and a doorway and a roof. The company put a telephone in the place, and a stool, and a small table on which Matt could rest his billycan of tea and cocoa until it was time to drink it.

Mrs. Dan Manning, who kept the gate lodge at "the castle," has described that billycan and its contents many times since she first filled it for Matt Talbot.

The can, she says, was made of tin; but the cap was of enamel, and, as it wasn't made for the can, it didn't fit very snugly. Matt put cocoa into the can, then a pinch of tea. Mrs. Manning poured boiling water into the impossible mixture — Matt implored her always to see the water was properly boiled, and once he had complained that she forgot to do so. Then she put the cap on and gave the can to Matt, or left it where he would find it. Matt always waited until the liquid had lost all sense of temperature. When he finally drank it — to wash down the dry piece of bread he allowed himself during the noon hour — it was not only nauseous but dead.

The office, in time, became a sort of oratory. Matt would retire into its gloom and privacy, to pray. He was interrupted frequently by the Manning children playing in the yard — who loved his stories of saints and angels — by orders for wood coming on foot or over the telephone wires, and by lorries driven up for loads.

66

Matt took a long time to get used to the rudeness and the shrillness of the telephone, the imperative call of it, the relentless servitude it exacted. But then, that was the way the world was nowadays.

Tremendous things were happening in that world — tremendous to other people if not to Matt. The English had fought a war with some people called Boers. Victoria had died. Railroads were being built everywhere in the world, and the speed of the trains increased every day. Steamboats were a common sight. The Yankees had invented many things, including the strident phone — movies, electric lights, gramophones, automobiles, motorcycles, even airplanes and crystal radio sets.

Matt heard of all these things from the talk of the men in the yards, but he wasn't much interested in them. When somebody was talking about balloons, for instance, or horseless carriages, or the way things had happened at Khartoum or Ladysmith, Matt would be wondering what had made Brother Furlong so happy this morning, or when the Pope would canonize the dear Little Flower, or how he could more clearly tell the Virgin the joy it was to belong entirely to her.

He lived in two worlds. He lived parsimoniously in one, in poverty that verged on destitution, in constant hunger and thirst, in clothes few beggars would put on, in constant work and constant prayer and constant fight against any tendency to sleep, in constant unconcern for the so-called progress of the age, and in constant concern for the souls of those around him.

But in the other world he knew excitement and splendor and ecstasy and tranquillity, and something of the progress of his own soul toward its destiny, Perfection. He knew the excitement and the splendor so well it showed through his eyes, even as he listened to men talking of the Spanish-American War, or the latest type of machine gun, or the possibility that submarines might play a little part in the next war, or the fact that labor unions were getting stronger and stronger in America.

Matt's intimates must have thought, when they thought

67

of him at all, that he lived a bleak, drab, monotonous, miserly, dull, and empty sort of existence. No liquor. No tobacco. No movies. No shows of any kind. No newspapers. Nothing but Church and the missions.

And, undoubtedly, Matt must have wondered how normal, healthy, intelligent, Christian men could lead such shallow, commonplace, unimaginative, mediocre, sterile, unblessed lives — why they should seek the pleasures of the world, which were not even the shadows of the joys to come.

Why did they not know that life comes to those who die to themselves — abundant life? Apparently they didn't want even to think of such a thing. They regarded self-denial as rank folly. Penance and mortification? Matt didn't venture to discuss such things with them, lest he evoke their mockery on these tools of grace.

The world was going faster and faster away from Christ. It got richer and wiser all the time. It shrunk space between far cities. It conquered the land and the air and the sea. It produced more leisure and more ease and more luxuries for the idle and the comfortable and the rich; and it produced more drunkards, more beggars, more criminals, and more maniacs all the time. It made gods of industry, commerce, education, and the various sciences, and made no god at all of Christ.

And all the while eternity was spinning toward the earth and everybody on it and so few people cared, or worried, or made the least preparation for the impact. They had ears that heard not, eyes that did not see. How could one warn such people? How could one show them the right highroad to progress, the only progress that would matter, the progress toward the judgment seat of God?

It was St. Louis Marie de Montfort who gave Matt Talbot the information he had sought so long in the pages of so many books, St. Louis who had died 140 years before Matt Talbot came into this vale of tears.

"Predestinate soul," St. Louis said to him, through the medium of a small cheap pamphlet translated into English from its original seventeenth-century French, "here is a secret the Most High has taught me, which I have not been able to find in any book, old or new. I confide it to you by the inspiration of the Holy Ghost. . . ."

It was the *Secret of Mary.*

Matt read in amazement, in delight, in growing inspiration, the things St. Louis had written in that book, and its companion book, *Treatise on the True Devotion to the Blessed Virgin.*

The saint had learned the secret in the School of Love. He had learned it from such masters as St. Augustine, St. Thomas, St. Bernard, St. John Eudes, St. Bonaventure, and St. Francis de Sales, and from such sources as Mary and her Son, Love Itself.

Matt read with swelling heart and shining eyes the love words written of the Mother of Fair Love. "The living mold of God" . . . "The sweets of the cross" . . . "the city of God" . . . "the sole treasurer of the treasures of the Most High, and the sole dispenser of His graces."

To go to Jesus, he learned, we must go through Mary. She is our mediatrix. That is the secret. God has to form great saints for Himself, saints "who shall surpass most of the other saints in sanctity, as much as the cedars of Lebanon outgrow the little shrubs. . . ." He wants to form these souls through Mary. She will be the mold of these great saints, even as she was the mold of Jesus.

These great souls [St. Louis predicted], full of grace and zeal, shall be chosen to match themselves against the enemies of God, who will rage on all sides; and they will be singularly devout to our Blessed Lady, illuminated by her light, nourished by her milk, led by her spirit, supported by her arm, and sheltered under her protection, so that they shall fight with one hand and build with the other.

With one hand they shall fight, overthrow, and crush the heretics with their heresies, the schismatics with their schisms, the idolaters with their idolatries, and the sinners with their impieties. With the other hand they shall build the temple of the true Solomon, and the mystical city of God — that is to say, the most Holy Virgin, called by the holy fathers the "temple of Solomon" and the "city of God." By their words and their examples they shall bend the whole world to true devotion to Mary. This shall bring upon them many enemies; but it shall also bring many victories and much glory to God alone. It is this which God revealed to St. Vincent Ferrer, the great apostle of his age. . . .

It is by Mary that the salvation of the world was begun. It is by Mary that it must be consummated. . . . God wishes to reveal and discover Mary, the masterpiece of His Hands, in these latter times. . . . As she is the aurora that precedes and reveals the Sun of Justice, Jesus Christ, she ought to be recognized and perceived in order that Jesus may be so. . . . Being the way by which Jesus came to us the first time, she will also be the way by which He will come the second time (though not in the same manner will He come the second time). . . . Being the sure means and the straight and immaculate way to go to Jesus Christ and to find Him perfectly, it is by her that the holy souls who are to shine forth especially in sanctity have to find our Lord.

He who shall find Mary shall find life; that is, Jesus Christ, who is the Way, the Truth, and the Life. But no one can find Mary who does not seek her; and no one can seek her who does not know her.

One who wished to be a great saint must consecrate himself and all that he was and might become, and all that he had and might be given, and all his good actions, and every grace or reward his good actions might merit from on high, "to Jesus in Mary."

That was a phrase Matt Talbot loved, *To Jesus in Mary*. It was as delightful as the words of St. John Eudes, "Jesus, Heart of Mary!"

A man must consecrate himself fully to Jesus in Mary, let Mary take complete possession of him so that she might dispose of him, and of his spiritual riches, "according to her good pleasure." A man must become a slave to Jesus in Mary if he would be a great saint. He must be bound in holy chains, in chains of love, if he would indeed be free. A man must be a slave and give himself fully to the guidance of the Virgin, who would some day introduce him, and all his virtues, to her Father, her Spouse, and her Son.

Sometimes it seemed to Matt that the great saint, who had learned so many things in the hard school of love, was talking directly to him.

> . . . The power of Mary over all the devils will break out especially in latter times, when Satan will lay his snares against her heel; that is to say, her humble slaves and her poor children, whom she will raise up to make war against him. They shall be little and poor in the world's esteem, and abased before all, like the heel, trodden underfoot and persecuted as the heel is by the other members of the body. But in return for this, they shall be rich in the grace of God, which Mary will distribute to them abundantly. They shall be great and exalted before God in sanctity, superior to all creatures by their animated zeal, and leaning so strongly on the divine succour, that, with the humility of their heel, in union with Mary, they shall crush the head of the devil and cause Jesus Christ to triumph. . . .

The little ones! The humble ones! The slaves! Ordinary people like himself! They could become saints, extraordinary saints. They didn't have to be priests, or lay brothers, or nuns. They could be workmen smelling of creosote, or guano, or tar, or wood, or bricks and mortar. They could be ex-drunkards. They could "know the grandeurs of the Queen and consecrate themselves entirely to her service as subjects and slaves of love." They could "deliver themselves to Mary, body and soul, without reserve, that they may thus be all for Jesus Christ."

To Matt this was a greater discovery, and a greater boon to mankind, than radio or any other wonder of the age of wonders. It gave him heaven, since it made him Mary's. He could hardly wait to consecrate himself to her, giving her "the entire and full right of disposing of me, and all that belongs to me, without exception, according to thy good pleasure, for the greater glory of God, in time and in eternity."

He could hardly wait to load himself with chains, the symbols of his sweet and holy bondage.

He was beginning to travel as fast toward Christ as the world was speeding from Him.

# Part II

# The Words of an Archbishop

"The exaltation of the lowly and the glorifying of the humble were new and characteristic doctrines of the religion whose divine Founder was born in a stable and died, stripped of all reputation, on the tree of shame. . . .

"The faithful are aware that a popular devotion has already grown up and spread far beyond the limits of our diocese and country, the object of which is a working man, named Matthew (or familiarly Matt) Talbot, whose lonely death . . . gave little indication of the fame which, in a very brief space of time, was to make his name and story known in almost every country in the world. . . .

"It seemed that the hand of Providence must surely be here, and that God had chosen one of our own beloved poor to show forth to the world the working of the ever abiding principle of holiness which is in the Catholic Church. . . .

"We earnestly exhort the faithful to pray that the guidance of the Holy Spirit may direct our steps, and that God may be pleased to add the name of His humble servant, Matt Talbot, to the glorious roll of Ireland's saints. . . ."

(*From the pastoral letter of His Excellency, the Most Rev. E. J. Byrne, D.D., archbishop of Dublin, dated November 1, the Feast of All Saints, 1931.*)

# 9

SHORTLY after he had placed himself under the tutelage of St. Louis de Montfort, and had begun to attend morning and evening classes in the School of Love, Matt Talbot was given an opportunity to practice what he had learned, and thus to perfect himself in the study and the love of Jesus in Mary.

This was arranged through the malice of the Prince of Darkness and some of his fat friends; but not in any conscious effort of giving Ireland another saint to add to her calendar of saints.

The lord of the bottomless pit cannot create, as God does. And, being infuriated at his impotency, he befouls, despoils, degrades, debases, corrupts, rips apart, destroys, or kills — whenever he is permitted to do so.

For many years he had been preparing a special sort of hell on earth for the Irish, the fools who still loved Christ and Mary despite all the devil had done to them. And he had been preparing well, exciting the avarice of the powerful and rich, increasing the despair and the envy and the anger and the debauchery of the weak and poor.

History speaks of this visitation as "the great Dublin strike and lockout of 1913."

One historian, Seamus O'Brien, writing in *Dublin's Fighting Story,* describes the people of the city as a silent, bitter mass "living in the most abominable hovels of any European city, working for a mere pittance, only sufficient to keep body and soul together, without the right or the power to demand any decent conditions or any protection from the harshest and most overbearing accumulation of masters ever gathered together."

The average weekly wage of the laboring man, he states, was sixteen shillings, about $4. There were many, however, he admits, who worked for much less, and there were some women whose employers paid them anywhere from one shilling to four.

> The hours of work [he writes] were 60 to 84. Dismissals took place without any reason being given. Foremen and managers used their positions of power to the utmost. . . . On the docks men scrambled for the day-to-day jobs offered by the stevedores. The unemployed labourers turned to the riverside for the chance of a few hours' work. Wages were paid in the snugs of the public houses in the vicinity — the stevedore collecting his rakeoff from the publican for the trade secured by his patronage. Woe betide the man who dared turn away and bring his wages home in full. . . . He was blacklisted . . . he walked the quays until he learned that he must leave a portion of his wages in the public house.

The devil was using his old tricks again with bread and wine. Matt, absorbed though he might be, in the things of heaven, could not but see the things of hell as he walked through the filthy streets to work and back again. Conditions were a little worse than they were in 1868 when he got his first job, and his first man-sized drink. The archfiend had been allowed to work peacefully through the years, feeding the fat on the bread of the thin, adding weight to the vicious at the expense of the wives and children of the workmen, increasing the destitute to shameful numbers.

Christ "in the least of these" was underpaid, overworked, shackled, shamed, scourged, and crowned with the thorns of seeing His women in the dirty streets — some of them with the innocence of childhood still in their furtive eyes.

And things would be getting worse rather than better, though no man would think they could get worse — even with the help of the devil.

But there was Sir Edward Carson, in Belfast, arming the Ulster Volunteers, with the connivance and the blessing and the secret help of English politicians and such men as Sir Henry Wilson of County Longford, and Field Marshal Lord Roberts himself. It was against Home Rule for Ireland Sir Edward was — though all the rest of the nation seemed to want it. And he had the guns, freely given, though it was against the law. The divil a hand in England was raised to stop him. There was a campaign of hatred being waged up north too, hatred against Catholics and all they stood for. It was being drilled into the poor Protestants, even the most peaceful and kindly of them, just as the use of the rifles was drilled into the marching squads of would-be soldiers.

Wisha, there was war and religious hatred simmering in the north; and there was war and bigotry and intolerance and pride and desperation and bloody murder stewing here in Dublin.

There would soon be armies drilling in the south of Ireland, to meet the Ulster menace, despite all that foolish and complaisant politicians might say to the contrary. Let them talk about Ulstermen handling only dummy guns and how ridiculous it was. There were patriots who were sad. Listen to the answer of Padraic Pearse, the founder of a Catholic school for boys and a Catholic school for girls. Pearse wasn't happy. "Personally," he said, "I think the Orangeman with a rifle is a much less ridiculous figure than a Nationalist without one."

There was another schoolmaster, Eamon de Valera, who

felt the same way about it. He was getting ready, like Pearse and many others, to fight and die for Ireland if the occasion rose. There was nothing much to lose. Life wasn't of great value under these intolerable conditions. But there was something wonderful to gain — an Ireland free at last.

Wars and rumors of wars! And there were dark clouds over the labor world. Jim Larkin, the big, turbulent, eloquent organizer of workingmen, was sounding the trumpet of the rights of man, and preaching the strength and holiness of brotherhood and union.

A Catholic bishop had referred to Larkin as "Antichrist," but Matt could not reconcile his words with those that came from the tender lips of Pope Leo XIII which told the workers they had the right and the duty to strike for just wages, if they could obtain them in no other way.

Jim Larkin had organized the dock workers and other laboring men. He had forced the bosses and the petty-thieving foremen to quit paying the men in barrooms. He had made some men free of liquor and thieves and want. He had corrected other abuses in the hiring and firing of men and women. He had been harassed, vilified, damned, persecuted, jailed, discredited, falsely accused, and threatened. But his power grew. And the strength and the love of little men grew with him.

And so, inevitably, when the devil was ready, the tragedy began. The men of the Dublin Steampacket Company went on strike. The employers resorted to the "lockout" and the importation of nonunion men. The four hundred principal employers of the city, the Sanhedrin, the council of the high priests of industry and commerce, met immediately and issued drastic orders.

All union men must, peremptorily and forthwith, give up their unions. All others must pledge themselves under penalty of immediate dismissal and eternal black-listing never to join a union.

Perhaps Matt Talbot sighed. The long-deferred issue was presented to the men of Dublin. What would they do? Would they bend the knee to insolence and emptiness and vanity and avarice and ungodly power? Or would they sacrifice themselves for justice, for their fellow men, and for the future of their wives and children and their holy Faith?

Blessed are the meek, Christ had said. Blessed are they that mourn. Blessed are they that hunger and thirst after justice. Blessed are they that suffer persecution for justice' sake.

The men went valiantly forth, to suffer and to fight for justice. The Sanhedrin decreed a general lockout. It was expedient, its leaders felt, that the people should die of hunger rather than the temple of business show a loss of profit.

"Most of these men had no strike funds to fall back on," said George Russell, better known to literature as AE. "They had wives and children depending on them. Quietly and grimly they took, through hunger, the path to the Heavenly City. . . . Nobody has praised them, no one has put a crown about their brows: Yet these men are the true heroes of Ireland. . . . For all their tattered garments I recognize in these obscure men a majesty of spirit."

Dublin Castle, which was neither a castle nor a Dublin institution, summoned large bodies of peelers, the military police, the men of the Royal Irish Constabulary. These men had been organized some years previously by Sir Robert Peel to find out everything possible about every man, woman, and child, in the Emerald Island, and to report it to Dublin Castle. They went about heavily armed, and heavily fortified with usquebaugh and raw poteen. (One needs to keep oneself half stupefied with drink, in a land where he is despised and hated even by the children. Otherwise he might begin to hate and despise himself.)

The devil had but to hiccup now, to start the crucifixion.

Matt had no grievance against his employers. He had never had any trouble with them. If they had never given him a raise, it might have been because he never bothered to ask for one. They had given him certain privileges, however. And they had treated him well. He had had words, now and then, with some brash foreman, but then, who hadn't? And he had berated one because of his stinginess in giving to a charitable cause. (But he had apologized to the bewildered man the next day, saying the Lord had bidden him to do so.)

There were times when Matt had been given a bonus of a few shillings which he hesitated to accept, not believing he had any actual right to the money. Oh, the Martins were all right.

But when the time came, he put aside his tools and walked off the job to join his striking brothers. Matt saw Christ in the workers, in every one of them. Christ had been a worker, was a worker now, would always be a worker while the world existed. He saw Christ in the poor also, in the sick, in the women and children of the locked-out, the dispossessed.

Matt left his work, but he made it clear he would not join any picket lines. His friends didn't exactly understand his motives for refusing this stern duty; but "it was like Matt," they acknowledged, and they did not hold it against him. He would get the same strike pay, they voted, as those who did picket. His mother was sick. And Matt could use what little the union could spare, even if he could only buy a piece of ice with it to ease his mother's fever.

Christ, in the poor of Dublin, was to be crucified on the hard cross of long hunger. He would be suffering a long time before any lance could pierce His heart.

And it was Matt's task to stand beneath the cross, and watch and pray, that he might the further perfect himself in the School of Love, and in the Secret of the Virgin Mary.

It was an awful place for any man to be, there in the mob at the foot of the cross. One met the devil there, and many of his adopted children. But it was a holy place too. For the Son of God was there; and Mary, His Mother; and St. John — the only one of the twelve whose devotion never flinched nor faltered; and that wonderful girleen, St. Mary Magdalen; and the good thief; and maybe a half dozen others a decent man might speak to.

It was a terrible thing to see Christ hanging there, with the big nails sticking through His wrists and His feet. But it was glorious to note the looks He gave His Mother now and then, if a man were intelligent enough to read them. It was as though He were looking at His Father, and Himself, and the Crimson Dove, the Holy Ghost. It was as though God, looking into the mind of Mary, saw Himself. It was as though Father, Son, and Holy Ghost, met in her mind in one eternal act of love.

Man, man, it was a dreadful place to be. Yet what beautiful things a lad could learn there!

Mary, weeping for the Lord, loved every one of those who had engineered His passion and His death, the high priests, the scribes and the Pharisees, the soldiers, and all the poor mad people in the mob. Could any man learn to love like that?

It was not long until Matt had the opportunity to make a definite answer to that question.

There was a riot in the streets when nonunion men attempted to run the tram cars. The pickets attacked with violence, and many men were hurt. And a sorry Saturday followed that is remembered to this day, together with the Bloody Sunday it begot. The police charged into a crowd of unarmed, innocent people, men, women, and children, and beat them with batons, blackjacks, gun butts, and hard fists — and kicked the fallen with their heavy boots.

The attack came with sudden fury, killing two men, and injuring and crippling more than two hundred. Some who fled for safety into their wretched homes were pursued, and pummeled when they were caught. The peelers even tore down the holy pictures in certain tenement rooms, toppled the altars the pious had made for their private devotions — toppled and trampled them — and smashed the votive lights that burned before them.

It wasn't enough. The attack was repeated the following day, with greater fury, and against a greater crowd. This time more than six hundred men and women, and little boys and girls, were taken to hospitals when the fury ceased.

"We saw little girls ten years old with hair clotted with blood from broken skulls," wrote Tom Clarke, a patriot who

81

was to die willingly and proudly, "for God and Ireland," a few years later. "We saw an old woman with her nose smashed by a baton."

Mary, watching the rabble jeering her Son as He came forward with the heavy cross upon His bleeding shoulder, forgave them and loved them and prayed for them. She forgave and loved the men who had so thoroughly scourged her Son, and those who had put the purple robe upon Him to mock His kingship, and who had crowned Him with a crown of wicked thorns. She loved them and forgave them and prayed for them; even as she loved God and herself. That was her martyrdom — to love.

Could Matt forgive, and love, the Dublin Sanhedrin, and the scribes and Pharisees of its Chamber of Commerce who had so heartily congratulated the high priest on "his prudent firmness"? Could he forgive, and love, the savage peelers?

Could he forgive, and love, those men in Dublin Castle who so loudly deplored the ruthlessness of the police — after it had rested — and who so publicly washed their hands of all responsibility in this "unfortunate affair," and other "incidents" that might follow if the people persisted in their foolish and stubborn stand?

He must forgive every one of them. More, he must love them too, even as he loved his mother whose sufferings were multiplied by the strike and lockout. He must love them even as he loved himself.

Christ, hanging in hunger and thirst on this impossible cross, must see in Matt Talbot's eyes what He had seen in the eyes of His Virgin Mother — Himself, joined with the Father and the Holy Ghost in one eternal act of love.

On this one lesson in the School of Love depended Matt Talbot's sanctity and salvation.

To love or not to love. That was the question.

Matt spent most of his time during the lockout kneeling upright in the darkness of a church, praying for his friends and comrades, praying for his mother and himself, praying for his enemies and oppressors, and for all who hated and despised him, praying for ex-drunks like himself who had gone back to the bottle for confidence and courage, praying for a free Ireland, praying for a country where men and women could praise and love and honor Christ and Mary in security and peace.

He offered up his bread for friend and foe — the bread he had sacrificed when he walked out of the lumberyard. And he offered up the wine — the blood spilled on the street and the sidewalk and the curbstone, the blood of gentle victims, the blood he would willingly have shed from his own heart.

And those ruffians who had invaded the mean houses of the poor, to make scraps of the pictures of our Lady and the Sacred Heart . . . cheap chromos they would be, no doubt, and hideous with bright reds and greens and blues; but how dear to those who owned them! . . . those men who had been enraged by toy altars, and who had ground the chalk and plaster statuettes under their mud-stained, bloodstained, military heels . . . those men who had added sacrilege to massacre, who had assaulted God with as bitter glee as they had assaulted men . . . must he forgive them too? And must he love them also as he loved himself? Indeed he must.

"Father, forgive them for they know not what they do."

The path to sanctity was a rocky road. The trade, or the art, or the science, or the profession of love — whatever you wanted to call it — was difficult to learn. The gist of it was this — a man had to die to himself, and let the Lord and the Lady of Fair Love take full possession of him.

Let those fight who would. And let those talk and write and preach who could. Matt Talbot's part, his task, his martyrdom, his privilege, and the only role he was called upon to play, was to remain with Mary, to watch and pray, and to forgive and love.

An ex-drunkard, standing near an ex-prostitute and an ex-murderer and thief, and on fire with the same flame they had caught from Christ and Mary, might make a torch of himself to show his fellow men the Way.

# 10

MATT had played hooky as often as possible when he went to the Christian Brothers' school, and had left its classrooms forever as soon as he could. But he had no intention of quitting the School of Love, nor of taking a vacation from the daily lessons, difficult as they were.

There was nothing but strife, these days in Ireland; nothing but talk of Sinn Fein — "Ourselves Alone" — and drilling of young boys who would make a corduroy road to independence out of their own dead bodies, God and Mary willing; and threats of wars to come; and the continued bitterness of the strike and lockout.

"Cry aloud to heaven for new souls," AE cried aloud to the 400 soulless masters of the city. "You may succeed in your policy [of starvation] and ensure your own damnation by your victory. The men whose manhood you have broken will loathe you and will always be brooding and scheming to strike a fresh blow. The children will be taught to curse you. The infant being moulded in the womb will have breathed into its starved body the vitality of hate!"

This wasn't what Matt wanted. It wasn't what God wanted.

Big Jim Connolly, who had come from the United States to help Jim Larkin, made fiery speeches, rousing Irishmen everywhere to arm themselves against attack by the military police or the well-armed men of Ulster.

"You have been told you are not strong, that you have no rifles. Revolutions do not start with rifles. Start first and get your rifles after. Our curse is our belief in our weakness. We are not weak; we are strong. Make up your mind to strike before your opportunity goes."

The strike and the lockout ended, along toward Christmas of that tragic year, after nearly four full months of hate and hunger.

The Body of the Lord, the Body of Christ in the suffering people, was taken, finally, from the cross. The men went back to work when they could no longer bear the look of hunger in the faces dear to them. The employers barred but a few of them. The lockout disintegrated slowly, though nobody acknowledged this was so. The men were needed for the work at hand. They were not welcomed back. But they were not turned away.

Scarcely had Matt Talbot closed his ears to all the worldly talk around him, talk of guns and plots and stratagems and political intrigues and religious animosities, than he was forced to open them again and listen to the voices of rash rulers giving orders to begin World War I. And then there was the voice of John Redmond, the Irish Parliamentary leader, bidding the Irish Volunteers to doff their Irish uniforms and put on the British khaki; and the angry voices of the opposition leaders calling on the Volunteers to stay in Ireland and let John Redmond fight for Britain.

A home-rule bill — tailored to avoid offending Carson and his Ulstermen — had been placed on the Statute Book; but it would not operate until the war had ended. And perhaps the time and the method of its operation depended on what the Irish did about the war. John Redmond might have looked upon it as a brandished club, and feared it would fall heavily on Ireland if he did not heed its threat. Matt didn't know. Nobody knew.

But the other politicians had a chance to talk. And which of them ever lets that chance go by? Ireland must stay out of the war, they said. England might say she was fighting for the sanctity of small nations. England might weep great tears for bleeding Belgium, and for stricken Serbia. If she really cared so much for little nations, let her show some concern for little Ireland, bleeding Ireland, stricken Ireland. Stay out of it, young man. Stay home and make your own land strong. Let England perish if it be the will of God.

And there were those in Erin who muttered, as their fathers had done, and their grandfathers before them, "The devil fly away with England; the devil poison the land of England, and the waters around it and the sky above it; the devil break the bones of every Englishman."

There were others too, fine boys who had no wish to claim their inheritance of hate, who believed it was the knightly fight the Englishman was waging, who were moved by high ideals to volunteer for service overseas.

There was so much noise in the world of men, such a confusion of angry voices, such a din of cunning argument and impassioned oratory, such a clamor of opposite ideas, that a student of the School of Love could not endure it. Matt felt it a blessing that — due to his sleeping on a wooden pillow, or to the toll of the years — he did not hear so well as he used to. So much profanity he missed; so much gossip; so many lies; so many atrocious stories.

It was as though men all over the world were clapping their hands at the appearance of the devil, the carrion angel of war, and adoring him in all their native tongues. The more one listened to the voices of men the more imperative it became to listen to the voice of God, especially when it was speaking through the sweet lips of Mary.

There was fear in the young knights training for battle. There was also a great courage in them. And a high purpose. They felt it was a holy adventure opening up to them, in a manner of speaking, an enterprise in which a man might give up his life, ungrudgingly, for something he valued more than life. They were full of ideals. Yet the fear was not lessened in their hearts.

These were, perhaps, the days St. Louis Marie had seen when he wrote the little book about the woman with a mother's joys and a virgin's honor — the "more than perilous days."

"I foresee many ravening beasts which will come in a fury to tear this little book with their diabolical teeth . . . or bury it in the darkness and silence of a chest so that it may not appear," he wrote.

The book had been buried in a chest for more than a hundred years. But now all the world could read it and practice the devotion it recommended.

Those who read and practiced the devotion, the saint prophesied, would be attacked. "But what matter? Indeed, so much the better. The sight of those things encourages me and makes me hope for great success; that is, for a valiant army of brave soldiers of Jesus and Mary, of both sexes, to fight the world, the devil, and corrupted nature in those more than perilous days which are to come."

Perilous days or not, a lover might walk safely through them, even though the devil raged all around him. A lover who opened his heart to Mary, opened it wide to Father, Son, and Holy Ghost. Hence he was filled with love, and with the perfection created and overshadowed by that love. He dwelt in her and she in him. And where she dwelt, there dwelt the Triune God.

How could there be fear in any heart that had filled itself with Mary and with God?

The young men of 1914 were indeed embarking on a high adventure. If only they could learn what a sublime adventure one undertook when he embarked on the quest of sanctity —

87

when he set out to woo and win the immaculate daughter of the King!

Perilous days indeed. On Easter morning, in 1916, while Matt still knelt in his accustomed place in the Jesuit church, his body rigid and erect from the bare knees to the bowed bald head, a curious column of men passed slowly through the quiet sunny streets, bent on proclaiming the Irish Republic, and declaring war on England!

Some were in the uniform of the Irish Volunteers. Some wore ordinary clothes. If one looked closely he could not help noticing some uniforms were a dark shade of green, some a light shade. Nor could he fail to note that some men had rifles of different makes, some had shotguns, some had picks and axes and sledge hammers, and some had pikes. All had yellow arm bands. A horse cab full of guns and homemade bombs, and a dray laden with arms and ammunition, accompanied the slow cortege.

Jim Connolly, Patrick Pearse, and Joseph Mary Plunkett led the strange little army into O'Connell Street, halted the men in front of the general post office, and gave the orders that amazed a war-torn world.

Within a few hours, for the first time in Ireland's long history, an Irish flag waved over its capital. It was a beautiful green banner, bearing the words, in white and gold Celtic letters, "Irish Republic."

Within a few minutes after the rebels had captured the post office, and stationed themselves in other points of vantage, such as the Four Courts, and Boland's Mills, and the Turkish baths in Stephen's Green, the proclamation of the "new government" had been posted up; and the first British soldiers had been killed.

"Irishmen and Irishwomen," the proclamation began . . . "in the name of God and of the dead generations from which she receives her old tradition of nationhood, Ireland, through us, summons her children to the flag and strikes for her freedom."

Even before Matt had left the church after the last Mass

that glorious Easter morning, the first barricades had been erected in the streets.

Christ was risen. Aye, verily He was risen. And in His name, and in the name of His holy mother, a few hundred Irishmen hoped to summon Ireland from its musty tomb!

Roger Chauvire, professor of the National University of Ireland, writes but a few paragraphs about this "rising," in his *History of Ireland;* but what he writes is worth the reading.

> There was a new thought coming to birth among a small nucleus of the volunteers, a thought belonging to idealists and poets and not that of calculating men, but who, as things turned out, were to have a wider reach . . . than the calculators. Their leader was Patrick Pearse. . . . He was a Gaelic poet, the founder of a school . . . and he was convinced that this soft, drowsy Ireland, to whom they were always crying up the material advantages of Home Rule, must be woken up from her rumination, and her soul must be restored to her.

> This could be done in one way alone, the offering of blood; a small band of enthusiasts, or confessors, shall we say, would prove to the world, would prove to Ireland herself, that she was worth dying for. . . . This was a mystical conception, which to some may appear disordered and romantic, but it can be explained by Gaelic history and poetry, and also by Gaelic mentality; Pearse, and his companions, Plunkett and Mac-Donagh, were poets, while Connolly . . . was a theorist rather than a politician. Ireland might perhaps give but one cry, yet that one cry would, without tricks or shams, claim the whole of her rights.

The original plan was to open the battle on Easter Monday. But Sir Roger Casement, who had gone to see what help could be expected from the Germans, had been captured. There was no time to lose, Pearse thought.

"When I was a child of ten," Pearse said, weeks later, "I went down on my bare knees by my bedside one night and promised God that I should devote my life to an effort to free my country. I have kept that promise. . . . To refuse to fight would have been to lose. To fight is to win. We have kept faith with the past and handed a tradition to the future."

For a whole week the few hundred rebels withstood all the attacks of the British infantry, the shelling of the gunboat *Helga,* stationed in the Liffey, and the terrible effects of the artillery fire. They capitulated only when they were exhausted with the loss of sleep, when they were out of food and ammunition, and when they could no longer take care of their wounded nor properly bury their dead.

Matt heard many tragic stories during that furious week, despite his growing deafness. And he heard stories that made him think God still loved the Irish. The one about Eamon de Valera, now; that was a good one.

Dev was in charge of the fighting at Boland's Mills, and bitter fighting it was. And, bedad, one night, going the rounds, he found some sentry posts deserted. What was he to do? Shoot the poor omadhauns as deserters? Sure, he didn't want to do that. So he went looking for the fine laddybucks. And where was it he found them, do ye think? On their knees in a nearby hut, saying the Rosary, the beads in their hands, and their rifles stacked in the corner. It's Mary was guarding the posts that night!

And there was the one about the English soldier creeping close to the men in Stephen's Green one night to see what sort of shenanigans was going on, what sort of signaling it was the commander had heard.

It was a weird sort of code the Irish were using, he reported. One chap said something like, "Mystical Rose," and a dozen voices said something that sounded like, "Pray for us." Only, of course, it must be something else. Then the first chap went on again with his code words. "Tower of David," he said, "Tower of Ivory," and "House of Gold." Calling for artillery he was, from the towers and the house; and the others were passing the word along.

And there were many stories about priests anointing dying men and boys lying in the streets, or in the burning stores and houses. Matt liked those, especially that story about the priest who crawled into the general post office, during the worst of the bombardment, to hear confessions and do what he could for the wounded.

There was a young fellow there with a load of bombs made out of tin cans and bits of iron pipe; and with a heart full of curses. And there was another fellow that said to him, "Man, dear, suppose God should strike you dead for the words you're saying, and you with all them grenades on you — where'd you be? Go see the priest now and don't be bringing the anger of the Lord down on us."

They were all lovers of Ireland, these mad patriots, these praying heroes. And most of them were lovers of Mary too. God would be good to them. God would be good to Ireland.

The Easter Rising had been put down. The heart of Dublin was in ruins. There were hundreds of dead on both sides, and hundreds wounded. Pearse and Connolly and others, who had surrendered themselves after the fashion of soldiers, were held in prison, and would be put to death, not as prisoners of war but as "traitors."

Matt Talbot could not have been unaffected by the failure of the "Rising," nor by the fate of those who had fought so fiercely. They had volunteered to lay down their lives for their friends. They had loved much. Undoubtedly that fact would be weighed in their favor at the judgment seat — that and the pleas for mercy Matt offered up night and day, and his earnest prayers for peace, the peace God so readily gives His children, turning evil into good.

# 11

MATT prayed for peace, but it was not God's will to grant it immediately. There was a great sadness in the old man — he celebrated his sixtieth birthday the day before the first of the fifteen idealists were led out, handcuffed, to be shot — but he had learned there could be peace in sadness. Our Lady of the Seven Swords had taught him that.

It was sad that England should show no mercy to these defeated patriots. But there was balm in the knowledge that most every one of them died in the peace and the love of God. Some of the words they said, Matt thought, were such as only Christian men could utter.

"My object in agreeing to an unconditional surrender," Pearse said, "was to prevent the further slaughter of the civilian population of Dublin, and to save the lives of our gallant fellows, who, having made for six days a stand unparalleled in military history, were surrounded, and without food."

Matt Talbot had no qualms of conscience in asking God's

92

blessing on such nobility of spirit and such willing sacrifice. There would indeed have been much further slaughter of civilians he knew, had the fighting been prolonged. Matt had walked through the streets at all hours of the day and night, though it was unsafe.

One might go cautiously, avoiding the islands of light the feeble gas lamps made, staying far from the streets where the great arc lights sputtered — until some patriot shot them out — but there were snipers everywhere, and lorries scurried suddenly around dark corners, and machine guns fired. The soldiers fired first and asked their questions later.

"Be careful, Matt," he was advised. "With those wooden ears, you'll not be hearing anyone say, 'Halt,' or 'Who goes there!' Musha, you'll not even hear the bullet that'll halt you."

Pearse had known he would be put to death if he surrendered. Yet he surrendered. He did not run away. The city owed him much.

"I fully understand now, as then, that my own life is forfeit," Pearse told his judges, "and I shall die very cheerfully if I can think that the British government, as it has already shown itself strong, will now show itself magnanimous enough to accept my single life in forfeiture and to give a general amnesty to the brave men and boys who have fought at my bidding."

No wonder God loved men so! Even the worst sinners He loved. But a man like this! A young man willing to die for others! How much God must love this man — remembering that His Son too had offered and given up His life, that other men might live.

Connolly had been badly wounded in the fighting. But that didn't bring him any pity, save from his own. And yet, it seemed to Matt and to many others that it wasn't pity Connolly wanted — or needed.

He was permitted to say good-by to his wife. "Hasn't it been a full life, Lily?" he said to her, kissing her tears and acting as if it was she who were going away and not himself, "and isn't it a good end?"

93

A good end? Say rather a good beginning.

Tom Clarke made a prophecy before he died, and Matt lived long enough to know it would come true. "Freedom is coming," Tom said, "but not at once. Ireland will go through a very terrible time between now and the final blow. There will be another big fight. We all believe this, that Ireland will be free. And in that belief we all die happy."

Thomas MacDonagh wrote a few sentences to the wife he was not allowed to see; but it was the sort of love letter that gets around, in time, to millions of people. "I am ready to die, and I thank God that I am to die in so holy a cause. . . . I counted the cost, and am ready to pay it."

The letter was written on May 2, Matt's birthday, toward midnight. MacDonagh had been tried that morning, but it was not until late at night that he learned he was to die. He was shot at 3:30 o'clock on the morning of May 3.

Eamonn Ceannt wrote that he did not shrink from death at daybreak. "I hope to see God's face," he said, ". . . His will be done."

Joseph Mary Plunkett, who was recognized as among the best of the young poets in Ireland, was permitted to marry his fiancée in his prison cell.

The story, as told by John Brennan in *Dublin's Fighting Story,* was one that made Matt Talbot, and many other Irishmen, increase the ardor of their prayers for England.

He had been engaged to Grace Gifford since December [Mr. Brennan wrote], and it had been arranged that they would be married on Easter Sunday. . . . They agreed that if he were arrested, Grace would marry him in prison. Her brother-in-law, Thomas MacDonagh, had been executed in Kilmainham prison at 3:30 a.m. on May 3rd. That evening, at 6 o'clock, Grace was summoned to the same prison for her wedding.

Until 10 o'clock, when she was brought into the prison chapel, she walked up and down alone by a long wall, on the other side of which, she was told, Joe Plunkett was waiting. The gas supply had failed, and the prison chapel was lit by a single candle, held by an armed soldier. Soldiers with fixed

94

bayonets filled the little chapel, and as Father Eugene Mac-Carthy read the marriage service, two soldier witnesses shifted their rifles from hand to hand as they assisted at the ceremony.

Immediately afterwards, the newly-married couple were separated. Grace was taken away to lodgings found for her by Father MacCarthy, and Plunkett was led back to his cell. They met only once again. She was summoned to the prison just before his execution on the morning following their marriage. Fifteen soldiers with fixed bayonets stood by while they spoke in his cell. "Your ten minutes are up," said the officer in charge, glancing at his watch, and they parted for ever.

As Plunkett waited with his hands tied behind his back to be led to the place of execution he said to Father Sebastian, who attended him, "Father, I am very happy. I am dying for the glory of God and the honour of Ireland." He was shot May 4, 1916.

Ned Daly, Con Colbert, Sean Heuston, and the others — they all died with prayers on their lips, Matt Talbot learned. Ned Daly looked like a "young knight who had won a tremendous victory," his sister said, and he promised there would be "a glorious meeting in heaven." Con Colbert asked his people for prayers — prayers that he might die well, and they might bear the sorrow well. Sean Heuston died like a saint, according to the Capuchin priest who was with him, Father Albert. "He was perfectly calm," the priest said, "and he said with me, for the last time, 'My Jesus mercy.' I scarce had moved a few yards away when a volley went off, and this noble soldier fell dead. I rushed over to anoint him. His whole face seemed transformed and lit up with a grandeur and brightness I had never before noticed."

Fifteen were shot dead by the British in Dublin. One was executed in Cork. And another, Sir Roger Casement, was put to death in London. Nearly one hundred and fifty others were sentenced to penal servitude for long terms of years or for life.

Even the British couldn't stomach the soullessness of the executions. Sir Francis Vane, who was one of the British officers at the Portobello barracks, which had been savagely assailed by the rebels, said the executions had been carried out "in the most brutally stupid manner."

"The execution of three of the senior chiefs would have been adequate for justice," he said, "instead of (all these) being shot, one or two a day over a fortnight, culminating with the death of Connolly, a badly wounded man, (who was) taken out, tied to a chair, for he could not stand, and shot like a dog!"

George Bernard Shaw was another to protest at the horror. "The shot Irishmen," he predicted, would become martyrs and heroes to all their countrymen, "and nothing in heaven or earth" could prevent it.

And the bishop of Limerick, the Most Rev. Dr. O'Dwyer, in making a lament over the dead, could not refrain from voicing the thoughts of many peoples. Desmond Ryan, in *The Rising,* quotes him as follows:

> The Irish Volunteers were too few for the enterprise, but that is perhaps the worst that can be said against them. Rebellion, to be lawful, must be the act of the nation as a whole, but, while that is true, see the case of the Irish Volunteers against England. The very government against which they rose, and which killed them so mercilessly, has proclaimed its own condemnation. What is that ghost of Home Rule which they keep so safe in lavender on the Statute Book but a confession of the wrong of England's rule in Ireland? . . . Sinn Fein is, in my judgment, the true principle; and alliance with English politicians is like the alliance of the lamb with the wolf.

As if to sharpen the bishop's words, the English military began to act like ravening wolves let loose in a flock of sheep, with no shepherd and no shepherd dogs nigh to deter them. They crashed into private and public places, searching for "suspects." They had no warrants of any kind, but they needed none, apparently. The Englishman's home was his castle, they had been taught; but this wasn't England, and the people weren't Englishmen.

They enforced a curfew. And they arranged blockades and

cordons. When they sought some Irishman they suspected of being a patriot they went to extremes. They surrounded entire blocks of houses, and searched every room in every house, no matter how many innocent people they disturbed or frightened — or mishandled — in the process. They had no respect for hospitals, nursing homes, churches, rectories, stores, shops, schools, or private homes.

Armored cars kept rolling through the streets, machine gunners ready to spray death at individuals or groups, at the word of command. Airplanes circled angrily over the neighborhoods being searched, flying low and giving frightened women and children a glimpse of wicked power.

Sometimes the raids were made at night. Soldiers broke the doors with rifle butts when they were slow to open. Men, women, and children were made to get up out of bed — some being prodded by the ready bayonets. They were lined in the streets, the sick and the well, the cripple and the blind and the mother with the newborn babe, to wait there until His Majesty's men had finished searching the vacated tenements.

And always, it seemed, another boy was being hanged in the British jails. Or a group of them were bayoneted to death because they would not talk. Or their bodies were released to their relatives — who found them riddled with bullet holes.

Terror grew with terror. Irish youths by the thousands, by the tens of thousands, joined their fighting brothers, whether they could get uniforms or no. And guerrilla war soon flamed through all the countryside.

# 12

"IN ORDER to understand Matt Talbot, and how he felt about the terror during the days of the Black-and-Tans, and later during the civil war, you must know something about the Ireland of his day," says a nice old man now living in New York. "I can tell you some of the background. I was there. I was born in Ireland about the time Matt turned sober. I can tell you how he felt about all the murdering going on around him.

"The holy man must have felt, at times, like Moses coming down from the mountain, where he had been talking to the Lord God Jehovah, and seeing the children of Israel adoring the golden calf. Only, I'd say, Matt would be more sorrowful than angry with the Irish adoring the god of the gun.

"The anger in them, and the fear in them, and their distrust of England, and their belief that whatever they did they did for Ireland, 'the dark Rosaleen' — all that, as Matt knew, went back a long way in the Irish. It went back to the days of the arrogant and greedy landlord and his bailiff and his soldiers. And far beyond.

"But it took firm flesh in the days of the evictions. Ah dear, those were the awful days, and the awful nights. I saw some of them, and me no older than six or seven or eight. The peelers coming, and the landlord's agent with them, and the bailiff, and the great battering-ram that would soon be breaking the poor little house into rubbish! Sure, Stalin, or Tito, or the devil himself, couldn't do a better job of hate than that same battering-ram.

"It was pastures the landlord wanted, do you see? And no more farming in this particular place. He raised the rents so high the farmer couldn't pay. The eviction followed. It didn't matter to the landlord that the farmer and his people had lived in that poor little house and on that poor little farm for hundreds of years before the likes of him had ever heard of Ireland. All that mattered to him was that he could make more money raising cattle and shipping them to England than he could by growing potatoes or cabbages or beans. So the farmers had to go. And their houses had to go.

"You'd see, sometimes, ten or twelve families sitting on a hillside, the children clinging to their mothers and crying fit to break your heart, and an old man, maybe, staring at a broken crucifix, and an old woman without any teeth in her gums — I can see that one yet — looking up at the sky, and praying.

I remember a night when the rain fell, and it was cold, and the people had no place to go. No place at all. Their neighbors had been evicted too. And I know of children that died because of the rain that night, and the weakness in the legs of their fathers and mothers who couldn't carry them far along the road.

"It was then we began to hear of Captain Moonlight. He was everywhere. He was one that didn't turn the other cheek. Not he. It was the blade of a knife he turned, and it peeking through a landlord's ribs — or an agent's, or a bailiff's — and looking for the greedy heart. Or it was the muzzle of a gun he turned, this way or that. He waited for a moonlight night so that he could see the man he wanted to teach a lesson — and so that he could see well enough to get away.

"The peelers would know the next day, or the day after, which one in the neighborhood had played Captain Moonlight that particular night. They had ways of making a body tell. They boasted there was always an Irish informer to give them a murderer's name. And maybe they were right; but they didn't say what pressure they put on a man to make an informer of him.

"Many a bold Captain Moonlight was shot by the peelers, or strung up. But the landlords got to be a decenter sort, in time; and the agents weren't so quick with the battering-rams; and the bailiffs sometimes had other work to do than serve eviction warrants.

"Matt Talbot must have known all that, must have known that many a man told himself it was self-defense as he gave the knife the last little twist, or said a prayer for the black soul he was going to send into eternity with a discharge from his blunderbuss. Many a man held it wasn't murder at all, but sheer necessity. Many killed only because the English — whom they killed — had kept the priests and the schoolmasters from them. They didn't know it was sinful to kill, though it might be against the law. Well, it was against the English law — but who, in his right mind, wasn't against that law all the time? Ah poor Matt. He must have gone back up to the mountain top, sad for the people and for the country."

The Irish, hugging the bishop's words about Sinn Fein to their angry bosoms, and misinterpreting them, set about earnestly, after the slaying of the Easter heroes, to drive the English home. They set up a military headquarters in Dublin, organized recruiting squads, a counterespionage system, and select bodies of exterminators. One of these groups was known to initiates as "the twelve apostles," probably because they went about the city preaching and practicing the gospel of assassination.

The Irish studied their enemies, followed them, learned their habits, and planned the best time and the best way to stop their activities. They had to be sure of a man first. They must know he was a spy, a traitor, an informant, or an avowed enemy. Many an English secret operative, and many an Irish traitor, lived because the apostles were not sure of his guilt.

One night, in Dublin, fifteen enemy officers were killed by these quiet groups of counterspies, and four were wounded. The peelers reacted, to some extent, as the landlords had. Some resigned. Some discovered better jobs in England. Some went crazy. Some became more bloodthirsty than before. Some ran amuck with fear. To fill up their ranks, the British government recruited numbers of men recently released from the army — desperate characters, most of them, with a lust for killing.

They began work in their khaki clothes, because there was a shortage of Royal Constabulary uniforms. But most of them wore the black hat of the peeler. Hence the dog's name they were given. At the same time a group of army officers and ex-army officers, known to the Irish as Auxiliaries, was sworn in to assist the peelers.

Both forces, the Irish soon learned, were tough and strong. The Black-and-Tans, however, commentators declare, were far more relentless than the Auxiliaries, far more desperate, and far more atrocious in their work. It was the Black-and-Tans that burned the heart of Cork City in a drunken rage. The Irish, at that time, fled to the regular British army for protection. Furthermore, they were protected.

"There are English in Ireland," the nice old man in New York will tell you, "that are the finest people in the world. And there are English I wouldn't want to talk about. We didn't hate the English as English. We loved them. That we did. I went to school with a lot of English boys. We had to stay after school, for religious instructions, those of us who had the Faith. And every time this happened, the English boys would have the laugh on us. 'Fish and the pope,' they'd say, and wouldn't we fly at it then! Ah the bloody noses and the black eyes we gave each other! But all in love, mind you. All in love! When we came out of class, there would be the English lads, every jackeen of them waiting to play with us. We were inseparable.

"We hated nobody. We even loved some of the English ministers. My mother now, God rest her lovely soul, the time I broke my leg it wasn't the priest she thought of going to for help. It was the minister. And he kept me in a hospital for months, with all expenses paid, so that I walk without a limp today.

"There were some ministers, of course, that were different. During the famine, now, there were ministers wouldn't give a family soup unless they renounced their Faith. Sure we've long memories, we Irish. We don't forget the famine, though it's a hundred years ago and more behind us. And we don't forget the Protestant soup. To this day you'll hear people saying of this one or that other, 'His grandfather was a souper.' There's nothing more bitter an Irish tongue can say to some of the little ones than that — reminding them that in a moment of weakness and temptation one of their forebears traded his immortal soul for soup, while others starved gloriously to death."

Walking through the streets of Dublin "after he came down from the mountain," there were sounds and sights Matt Talbot could not help but see and hear — although his hearing grew constantly worse, and although he walked always, now, with his eyes cast down and his thoughts turned up. And many tragic tales must have been told him by his friends. Such tales, for instance, as the massacre the Black-and-Tans inflicted in retaliation for the wholesale assassinations.

It was, historians believe, a combination of fury, hysteria, and fear, that induced them to do what they did.

They decided either to burn all O'Connell Street, or to massacre the crowd watching a football match in Croke Park. They tossed a coin.

The Irish learned of the decision, but not soon enough to prevent it or to counteract it. Men went running to Croke Park to call off the match, to get the crowd to safety. The Black-and-Tans opened fire with rifle and machine guns, however, before the crowd was aware of any danger. There was, naturally, a panic. Many of those running away fell and were trampled upon. Some, trying to help the wounded, were

shot or bayoneted or clubbed. Hundreds were made to hold
their hands in the air for hours, before they were searched,
during the search, and long after the search was over. Fourteen
Irish men and boys were killed in that senseless onslaught, and
more than fifty were wounded.

And the keening women outside Mountjoy prison — Matt
must have heard of them if he did not see them himself. They
were there so often, while, within, some man or boy was
being put to death. Hundreds of women would be there, at
times, weeping, saying the Rosary, reciting litanies, some of
them with blessed candles lifted high, all of them begging
Christ and Mary to show mercy to their dear ones, to have
pity on the land that loved them so, and to bring back peace
to the world.

He must have heard men talking about the little bands of
Volunteers that raided British posts for guns and ammunition,
of the battles they fought against great odds, and the victories
they won, and the awful price they paid for victories.

And he must have heard stories that let him know our
Lady had not forgotten Ireland or the Irish. Some of these
stories have been told over and over again, especially by
priests and nuns — stories like these printed in the *Little Manual of Perpetual Help* by Cornelius J. Warren, C.Ss.R., Boston,
1921. . . .

The reader will recall those awful days of April, 1920, when
thousands of Irishmen watched at the gates of Mountjoy prison
while more than a hundred untried prisoners endured the
agonies of a hunger strike. All press correspondents agree that
during those days there was constant danger of desperate
slaughter in Dublin. Despite the barbed wire barricades, the
rifles, the ever circling planes of the military . . . despite the
efforts of priests and Volunteers to keep order, the maddened
crowd at times almost rushed on the soldiers in an effort to
reach their loved ones. . . .

One such rush would have meant that every rifle would have
spoken. . . . A picture of Our Lady of Perpetual Help, loaned
for the occasion by the reverend mother superior of the Mater
Misericordiae hospital, was carried in procession by ladies

right up to the prison door. Friends formed a circle around it and the Rosary was recited in Gaelic. . . .

On the evening of the eighth day, about 5:30, feeling reached a very ugly pitch. The first line of soldiers in the cordon fixed their bayonets and adopted a threatening attitude. Suddenly the church bell rang . . . the Angelus. Hats came off. A sudden silence fell. A tall young girl dressed in the uniform of the Cumann na Bann (the women soldiers) ascended a parapet overlooking the crowd and began . . . "The Angel of the Lord declared unto Mary!" Like thunder came back the response, "And she conceived of the Holy Ghost." Afterwards the girl soldier began the Rosary. . . .

We marched to all the churches and prayed for the prisoners. When word came they had been released we all went down to the Redemptorist church and made an act of Thanksgiving to Our Lady of Perpetual Aid. . . .

"Before me," says a Liguorian contributor, "is the photo of an altar erected in a prison. It is artistically decorated, but the structure is naturally poor, as it was built of whatever material lay to hand in a prison lumber room. In the center of the altar, over the tabernacle, is a large picture of Our Lady of Perpetual Help. This altar was erected by Eamonn De Valera and other prisoners. . . . After many months . . . the gates of the prison opened to De Valera and his fellow prisoners. It was the feast of Our Lady of Perpetual Help. . . . They knelt before her altar and said the Rosary to thank her for their deliverance."

The Sinn Feiners took over Ireland after the executions of the Easter heroes, established the Dail Eireann, the Assembly of Ireland, and once again proclaimed the Irish Republic. De Valera, who was in prison at the time, was named president; and he and most of the members elected swore not to have anything to do with the parliament in Westminster.

The British wouldn't have it that way. They gave Ireland the "Home Rule" they had withheld up to that time — and split the nation into the North and the South.

Irish Republic, or Irish Dominion, or Irish Free State, the ambushing, bushwhacking, raiding, and slaughtering went on. And the quiet assassinations.

Eventually, however, the Irish left off fighting the British to make a bloodier war among themselves. There were two factions, two armies, burning each other's strongholds, killing each other's men, each side convinced they were working for the good of the country.

" 'Tis good both sides love Ireland so," a Kerry philosopher said, looking at the charred buildings in a little town. "Think what they'd have done if they hated it."

It is possible that Matt was as well informed about the situation as any other Irish workingman of his time. But nobody, making exhaustive inquiries of his friends and acquaintances, ever learned that he had commented on it in any way.

Even of his own arrest and detention he did not speak.

The North Wall Hotel, one of the British army headquarters posts, was blown to pieces one morning while Matt was coming to work. The hotel was close to the Martins' lumberyard, and everybody in the vicinity was rounded up for "questioning." Matt was forced to raise his hands above his head, stand against a wall, and wait until his captors were ready to talk to him. He was searched, questioned, and finally released.

When people asked him about his adventure he parried their questions in his characteristic manner. "God is so good. Isn't it a pity more men do not love Him?"

Matt Talbot, standing beneath the cross beside the Lady of the Seven Swords, remained as silent as she did. If he had anything to say about his fellows, drunk with the blood of enemies and of brothers, it was but a prayer. The great charity that could encompass all the stew bums on Skid Row, all the derelicts in the third-rate hotels, and all the other alcoholic outcasts in the world, could embrace his fellow Irishmen and their enemies, and his, whether they battled rightly for the wrong, or wrongly for the right.

The hasty words he had said to his brothers, thinking to drive them from his father's house, the unkind things he had said in those days before he really knew the love of God and neighbor, the words for which he so often had begged penance and pardon of God, would have kept him silent about the events of the Rising, and of the scourge of the Black-and-Tans, and of the tragedy of the civil war. Remorse would have kept him from making comment if charity had not already sealed his lips.

He could have told his fellow men that the best way to conquer their enemies had nothing to do with bombs or bayonets or guns, nothing to do with strategies or raids or skillful ambushes or clever murders. He could have told them that the best way was to load one's self with the chains of the Virgin Mary and to go on one's bare knees and pray for them. He could have told them that the best weapon they could use was love — the love of Christ and Mary, and the love of their fellow men.

But Christ had told them that; and they had paid little or no attention!

Why should they listen to Matt Talbot? He was but a sinner himself, and, no doubt, a greater sinner than any of them. It was best to keep silent, and to watch and pray with Mary.

Peace or war, the will of God be done.

# 13

DURING the war, when employers had to raise wages to keep good workmen from the munitions factories, Matt's weekly pay was tripled. He had the equivalent of fifteen dollars a week. So he could afford, now and then, despite his tripled charities, to buy holy books to enlighten his mind, and heavier and heavier chains to bind about his body.

He was as secretive about those chains as he was about his charities, or his zeal for God.

It was not every boy Matt would tell how to fend off the gentleman with the fund of dirty stories; not every man he would show the crucifix, saying, "See whom you're hurting"; not every person with whom he would talk about religion.

One must not throw pearls to swine.

But no matter how carefully a man tries to hide his love from the world, he has no defenses when he meets one of his kind. Seeing another soul burning with adoration excites even the shyest lover of God so that he must reveal his love in all its shameless ecstasy. Thus he will stir his friend to further ardor, and his friend him; and both will be more pleasing to God, who is Love, than either would be alone.

It was only because he met kindred souls that Matt exhibited his chains. The first man he so honored was a bachelor who lived not far from his flat in Upper Rutland Street, and who probably went to daily Mass and Communion with him in St. Francis Xavier's Church. Sir Joseph Glynn identifies this man only as "J.G." — undoubtedly because J.G. was as shy as Matt and didn't want "just everyone" to know his secret.

> One Sunday [Sir Joseph says] Matt informed J.G. that he had read of a devotion which lifted him from earth to heaven . . . the wearing of a chain. . . . He showed a small chain wound round his leg. It was the same class of chain as was used to hang the weights of a clock.
>
> Matt lent J.G. the life of St. Catherine of Siena, and J.G. asked Matt if he had read in that life that St. Catherine wore a chain. He looked confused and said he supposed she did. J.G. then said that she wore it round her waist and that after her death it was found imbedded in her flesh, an exact parallel of what happened in the case of Matt Talbot himself. It was, however, the book of St. [Louis Marie] De Montfort which caused Matt to wear chains. He induced J.G. to wear a chain and brought him to Clonliffe College, where he had him enrolled in the chain by one of the priests.

The "clock-weight" chain gave way to the type used to restrain watchdogs. And this type was succeeded by chains that would hold a frisky calf, or even a good-sized bull.

He put them around his waist, around one arm, and around one leg. He put them around his shoulders too; but, since he had to carry lumber on those shoulders, and the chains prevented him from doing this well, he took them off.

He kept the chains on him at all times, until they became too rusty for further use. There were always new lengths waiting for him to bind about him. The rusty links he took secretly from his room and buried. Or he dropped them in the Liffey on his way to work when no one was looking.

108

Just as he hid his chains, so also he hid his other mortifications. Few of his friends guessed at his fasts, because when they asked him, now and again, to share their lunches, or to have dinner with them, he obliged with a willing smile. He even ate meat, on occasion, rather than let a friend suppose he was keeping any sort of diet. It might not only make a man ask questions if he refused the proffered food, it might also offend the fellow's hospitality. It was an act of charity to oblige such a friend — and charity is worth more than any act of mortification.

He hid his sanctity from everybody possible to hide it from. Perhaps only two men on earth, Father James Walsh, S.J., who is thought to have been his spiritual director, and the saintly Monsignor Hickey — who often came to Matt's room to remain there with him for hours, praying and singing hymns — knew there was anything like sanctity in the bald-headed little workman.

The priests at the Jesuit church, even those who so often gave him Communion, didn't know his name if they knew him at all. Even Brother Furlong, who saw him nearly every morning, and who admired him as a holy man, couldn't tell anything about him. The Franciscan priests, and the Franciscan tertiaries, who saw Matt often after he joined the Third Order of St. Francis, couldn't have given any sort of description of him, couldn't have told his name, wouldn't be certain they knew him if they met him on the street.

There was a Jesuit to whom Matt sometimes gave a five pound note, "for the poor," who would have sworn he never met the man — until after he heard about Matt's death. There was a collector to whom he also gave money for a statue of St. Therese, "the Little Flower," who didn't know the name or address of the donor. Matt liked to be as "anonymous" as any of his present-day friends in "Alcoholics Anonymous."

He lived alone, after his mother's death. He increased his austerities. He even put cinders on the floor of the office at "Castle Forbes" so that when he knelt, during the moments of waiting for lorries to arrive or for the phone to ring, his knees might rest on something less comfortable than the rough pine boards of the floor.

He had by this time established a prayer routine which included the fifteen decades of the Rosary, the Servite Rosary of Our Lady of Sorrows, the Franciscan crown of the seven joys of Mary, the Little Office of the Blessed Virgin, the Immaculate Conception chaplet, the beads of the Sacred Heart, and of St. Michael the Archangel, and of the Holy Souls in Purgatory, various litanies, various novena prayers, the prescribed prayers of the Franciscan tertiaries, and prayers that nobody knows anything about.

Work was prayer to him, the work of his body offered up to God for His greater glory. Work was prayer, and work was filled with prayer. Recreation was prayer too; and recreation, for Matt, was reading spiritual books, and writing, on scraps of papers, quotations from them.

"How is it you can understand a book like that?" Dan Manning once asked him, seeing Matt reading Newman's *Apologia*. Matt smiled and admitted he was an ignorant brute. But, he said, he prayed to the Holy Ghost, and to Mary, Seat of Wisdom, before he began any book. And, therefore, he managed to understand it — the gist of it anyway, if not all the big words.

He was not ashamed to confess that he had little learning. But he didn't regret the fact. God had made him the way he was, he said. God knew what He was about. God knew what was best, not only for Matt Talbot but for every other soul He had created. Some He had endowed with brilliance, with understanding, with genius. To some He had given quite different gifts. To Matt He had given the gift of prayer. Matt had asked God for it, he was careful to explain. He had begged for it, and God had given it to him "in great abundance."

Matt not only said prayers daily, he thought prayer, he lived prayer.

Reading spiritual books was prayer to him. Writing excerpts out of those books was prayer. Teaching the Manning

110

children bits of Catechism was prayer. Making them happy was prayer.

Matt went through an unvarying ritual with those children every Christmas. He lined them up for their presents, and then searched every one of his pockets for a sixpence, pretending, until the very last moment, that he had lost the precious gifts.

As the children increased in number, Matt's Christmas gifts had to decrease in value; but the boys and girls got just as much glee out of Matt's frantic search for threepenny pieces; and the fun lasted a little longer every year.

A man could pray even while taking the egg from underneath a cackling hen in the lumberyard, and going out of his way to bring it to Mrs. Manning, the owner of the chicken. Mrs. Manning once ventured to tell Matt he was welcome to all the eggs he found outside the coop. He thanked her, and talked about the saints, and kept on bringing the eggs to her. It was good to give up the eggs, especially as they looked so wonderful to his ever hungry body.

It was a prayer, an act of love, a joyful sacrifice, to deny his guts their rights — and to make sure some other tummy than his own benefited by his loss. Well could he advise a friend not to "study the guts," nor to go shopping for them. It took more than guts to starve the guts, he knew. It took love — love that was stronger than hunger or thirst, stronger than life or death — stronger even than hate.

Miss Kate Byrne was another woman who presented eggs to Matt. She was a daily Communicant like himself, and eventually he made a "slave" of her. Matt became acquainted with her through her dog. The animal always accompanied his mistress to the church. Matt used to pet him. He loved dogs.

"One Saturday in the early spring of 1924," Miss Byrne told Sir Joseph, "I called at his room in 18 Upper Rutland Street about 3 p.m., with a few eggs."

Matt had been in and out of the hospital by this time. His heart bothered him. He had had to relax many of his strict habits. He was old, and weak, and he had not long to live.

They sat and talked for hours. Matt spoke of our Lady and of his favorite saints. Miss Byrne was so fascinated she forgot the time. When she looked at the clock she was astounded to discover Matt had talked three hours. It had seemed to her only a few minutes.

It was in this conversation, she declared, that Matt said he had read, in the life of some saint, that it was good to remain kneeling during Mass. Thus one would not be distracted.

Before she left the visitor told Matt to be sure to beat up the eggs and add a bit of milk to them in the frying pan. Matt smiled, and said, "God bless you for your kindness." He waited until she and the dog had gone — then gave the eggs to a neighbor.

Only with those who loved God dearly was Matt at all confiding. He could talk to a few men, and to fewer women. He could bewail to his sister Susan the handful of people there were on earth who really loved God and His immaculate Mother. And sometimes he would say, "Oh, if I could only tell you of the great joy I had last night (or the other day) talking with the Blessed Mother!"

Yet sometimes, so filled with the love of God was he, that blazing words burst out of him.

To a woman who told him that her brother, in the United States, was lonely, Matt was almost rude.

"Lonely?" he said. "With our Lord always there in the tabernacle where any man can visit Him? Lonely? Sure, that's just plain nonsense!"

To a friend who complained of illness and who asked what doctor Matt would recommend, he said. "Go to the same Doctor I do; the Doctor always waiting for you in the tabernacle. Go to Him. Make a visit every day."

To a friend who had stayed home from the 6:15 Mass at the Jesuit church because "the weather was too bad for any man to step outside his door," Matt gave a stern rebuke.

"It is constancy God wants."

In one of the notes found in his room after his death, and treasured by the finder, were these words. "On the feast of the Seven Joys B.V.M., 22nd August, 1915, I, Matt Talbot, was present at twenty-one Masses."

It was only to "J.G." Matt spoke of this.

"Where did you attend twenty-one Masses?" his friend asked.

"At the Pro-Cathedral," Matt said.

"Arra now," J.G. put in, "that you did not, Matt."

"Don't get the idea," Matt said, "that I heard one Mass after the other. No. That I did not. Many Masses were being said at the same time. It is necessary only to have the intention of hearing them all to get the merit of hearing them. Though you're attending only the Mass being offered at the altar before you, you're attending all the others as well."

J.G. nodded. Anyone could hear twenty-one Masses that way any Sunday in the Pro-Cathedral. But leave it to one like Matt to point it out.

"One very great personal friend," Sir Joseph has related, "stated he once spoke to Matt Talbot on the danger of feeling any pride in his great spiritual gifts. Talbot listened very respectfully, and then simply said that he could not feel pride in anything he had done when he thought of the actions of the saints."

Some people were puzzled "as well as amazed," this friend said, "that a poor fellow like Matt could have set his mark so high and consistently worked up to it." He continued:

"The explanation seemed to me to lie in his clear logical mind. He was convinced that if the truths of revelation, as regards the Incarnation and Redemption, were accepted as true, there should be no limit to our service save the impossible. It was this view, in my opinion, that urged him on to his life of extreme penance and enabled him to persevere to the end."

Here is another little story told by Sir Joseph, which illustrates how wisely and skillfully Matt cast his pearls.

Amongst his friends was one who, though a lifelong total abstainer, had for 30 years been absent from the Sacraments. During a conversation with Matt Talbot on the question of temperance, the latter suddenly asked him about his soul. Matt spoke seriously of the danger his friend ran of dying without the Sacraments, and, eventually, made an appointment with him for the following Saturday afternoon, when he brought him to Holy Cross College, Clonliffe. After he had made his Confession, Matt introduced him to the Sodality of the Immaculate Conception, of which he subsequently became a prominent member. He was, several years later, killed by a fall into the hold of a ship on which he was working.

# 14

MATT was sixty-seven when he went to the hospital. He couldn't get up one morning for work. For the first time in his life he couldn't command his body to do the things he insisted it do. He knew, therefore, that he must indeed be sick.

He went to his usual Doctor, after he got out of bed; but it seemed to him that the divine Physician referred him to an earthly doctor. Matt didn't know any earthly doctors, but he had a friend who recommended one, and this man, a specialist, sent him to the Mater Misericordiae Hospital.

Matt took off his chains before he went to the hospital, and removed from his body any rust stains that might have visited him since the last time he had put on new chains.

At the hospital another doctor examined him. Matt's heart was not too good, he said. He needed rest, and plenty of it. He was given a cot in an upper-floor ward, on June 18, in the year 1923. And he was in such condition that the chaplain gave him the Last Sacraments on the evening of June 21.

Matt's body could laugh at him now, the body he had

treated with such tyranny. It could lie in bed all day, and all the night too. It could lie there, do nothing, and be waited on. It could lie there and have nuns come and ask what they could do, and nurses, and doctors, and the priest himself. It could sleep — but it could never make up all the sleep it had been forced to lose during the thirty-nine years of Matt's sobriety. It could rest on a soft mattress for the first time in nearly four decades — and there was nothing Matt's will could do about that. It wouldn't have to get down on its marrowbones again until the doctors gave Matt the right to take charge of himself again. It wouldn't have to subsist on dry bread and that horrible goo made of tea and cocoa and boiling water that was allowed to get stale and dishwater cool before drinking. It could eat anything, thank God. Anything!

The body could jeer at Matt, but it was in pain. And so Matt could jeer in return.

"You thought I was severe, did you?" he could say. "Now you see how easy I was — now that you feel the powerful hand of God. Give thanks for the pain. You can offer it as a wonderful gift to our Lady. She can use it to help the sufferings of other poor sinners like yourself. She can use it to help the souls in purgatory. Sure, it's many things herself can do with the little pain God let you have. Give thanks for the gift of pain, and for the touch of the hand of God."

A few weeks after the priest anointed him, Matt was discharged from the ward, but was told to return to the hospital every day, if possible, for at least a month.

In mid-August he thought he was well enough to go back to his office at Castle Forbes, to handle the lumber as usual. But he was weaker than he knew. After two weeks he had to quit again. And at the beginning of October he was once more a patient in the hospital.

"You see," his body must have said, "you've overdone it, Matt, me fatheaded master and mortal enemy. You've starved me, chained me, overworked me, denied me sleep, tried to make me nothing but a kneeling bench for your will. And look what happens. Go on now, say your Rosaries all you like, it's me that'll be catching up on my rest. 'Tis a misery for you, Matt Talbot; but a holiday for me."

Matt stayed in bed until sometime in the middle of November. He was anointed again. And again the Sacrament intended for the dying seemed to put new life into him.

"I sent for his sisters," the nurse in charge of the ward said, "and told them he was dying. I thought it was good he should die then, he was so well prepared. I now think he may have been in a state of profound recollection. Two days later he was able to go downstairs to have a cardiograph taken. . . . The first day he was allowed up he disappeared. . . . I thought he had gone out and got an attack in the street. He was in a corner of the chapel praying. When I complained . . . he replied with his usual quiet smile, 'I have thanked the nurses and the doctors, and I thought it only right to thank the great Healer.' "

That must have been a triumph for Matt. He was master again of his body, forcing it anew to its knees to thank and adore the God who made it, and he knew that, though said body might trouble him a lot because of feebleness and age, he would remain in control of it until it died.

The Sisters noticed nothing unusual about Matt while he was under their care. Had anyone told them he was a saint, or even called him a saintly character, they might have smiled. (Sisters are polite; they never "give anyone the raspberry.") He was just a nice old man to them, a sweet old character.

Oh sure, they said, he received Holy Communion every Monday, when it was usually administered, and every other day when some kind nurse thought to ask if he would like to receive. He made no demands. He asked for nothing.

He was in our Lady's hands. If she saw fit, she would let him receive the Body and Blood of her Son. If she saw fit, she would give him the chance to make a sublime offering — the sacrifice of his own will to receive that Body and that Blood.

To one who loves God it is painful to miss Communion. But he sanctifies this pain — the terrible pain that comes from the absence of God — by accepting it. And he is richly blessed by offering it, through the Immaculate heart, to Love Incarnate and Divine.

He was blessed if he received. He was blessed if he did not. He could not lose. How can anyone lose who lets God's Mother guide him, who trusts himself completely to her will, which is the will of God?

He was too weak to return to work after he was discharged the second time, and he had to keep coming back to the hospital, if only for medicine from the dispensary.

He could get no money from the lumber people. They had no pension funds for aged and sick employees. He did get a few coins from his union, under the National Health Insurance Acts, but not very many. He drew twenty-six weeks' sickness benefit at the rate of fifteen shillings a week, a total of nineteen and a half pounds (a little less than $100 at that time) to pay his hospital bill. Thereafter he had to subsist on seven shillings and sixpence a week — which would almost equal $1.88.

Poverty didn't daunt Matt Talbot, nor illness. As soon as he went back to the old routine, he got up in time for 6:15 Mass in St. Francis Xavier's. He didn't get up at 2 o'clock, perhaps; and he wasn't able to wait an hour or more on the steps before the doors were opened; but he got there on time, and he got home again.

Sometimes he collapsed on getting home. His sister Sue came in one morning shortly after Matt had returned from the hospital, to find him lying on his plank bed so exhausted he could not speak.

"The walk was too much for you," she said. "You might have killed yourself going to church." He didn't answer her.

Sue made a substantial breakfast for him. He ate it. And presently he was ready to go back to the church to attend a later Mass.

"Someone ought to stay here and take care of you," Mrs. Fylan cried out. "The way you carry on! Have you no mercy on yourself? Suppose something should happen to you?"

"What good could you do, staying here?" he replied. "If I die, and there's nobody around, I'll still have Jesus and Mary with me."

He stayed on in the drab little room, sometimes too ill to do anything but lie on his planks and think of Those he loved; sometimes strong enough to move about. He couldn't always steal out in the dark of the morning to greet his Lord before the dawn. When he could, he enjoyed it more than before.

Over a year he spent thus, in feebleness and pain, and in solitude unbroken save for the visits of his sisters and a few old friends, and now and then a priest carrying Christ upon his breast.

At times he seemed to be his old self, to be back in the old routine of penance and worship — penance and worship but no hard work.

Many people were good to him during this period, people he didn't know, people who scarcely knew him. He wasn't Matt Talbot to them. He was just a poor old man who was doing his best to live on "seven and six" a week and not grousing about it. He was an object of charity. He was someone to help.

"He needs clothes," a group of women told one of the Jesuits. "But I suppose he's stubborn. You talk to him, Father. We'll buy the clothes. The poor old man — he's so nice, and so shabby! And his clothes are so thin! How can he stand it in weather like this? We'll get him good clothes, Father. The best."

Matt listened affably to the priest, but insisted he didn't want the clothes. He had no false pride. He had worn castoff clothes for years, taking the hand-me-downs of a number of old friends, and giving lavish thanks and fervent prayers for them. But new clothes? That could not be. God would never send new clothes to the likes of him.

"I promised God I would never wear good clothes," he told the priest. "How can I break my promise?"

"God is sending you the clothes," the priest pointed out,

"which indicates He wants you to wear them, promise or no promise."

"All right," Matt said, docilely. "If God sends them, I'll take them."

He could wear them, or he could give them away. He often gave away clothing that had been given him, but only when it was good enough to give away. The poor should have the best, the finest.

He also gave away money with the careless and happy extravagance of a prince on a honeymoon. It didn't matter that his income was only $1.88 a week. He lived on a few coppers, so he had plenty to disperse. He placed his money under one of the books on the chair. His sister who kept house for him knew where it was. Every once in a while she would count it, and ask what he wanted done with it.

"Glory be to God," Matt said one day, "where did all that money come from? Sure, sometimes, Sue, I think our Lady drops it down through the ceiling. I can't account for it in any other way."

It went to a priest in some dark confessional — "to be given to the poor, Father." It went to friends in need. It went to the Maynooth mission in China. It went many other places. Matt once stated he had sent thirty pounds sterling a year ($150) to the Maynooth mission; and he remarked to his sister that he had "finished three priests and was now on the fourth." It didn't take much money, comparatively, in Matt's time, to educate priests for the China missions, and to send them forth equipped. At least Matt didn't think it very much.

During his prolonged illness Matt wrote his first and only letter. This was in December, 1924. It was written to the friend who usually forwarded Matt's donations. It is a classic of its kind. It has been reproduced in a number of books. It bears reproduction in many more.

"Matt Talbot have Done no work for past 18 months i have Been Sick and Given over By Priest and Doctor i Dont think i will work any more there one Pound From Me and ten Shillings from my Sister."

120

Out of his $1.88 a week he had saved $5 for this one charity. The ten shillings, Susan said, Matt paid in her name. It was his way of "recompensing her" for the care she had taken of him during his long illness.

In April, 1925, with the feel of spring in the air, Matt decided he was well enough to go back to work. He was welcomed heartily by all his friends. They made much of him, and they made his work as easy for him as they could.

He looked much older than he was, even to the least observant of them.

They knew he was not nearly so strong as he appeared to be. They seemed to realize he had scarcely two months to live.

# 15

ONLY a few glimpses of Matt's illness and inactivity have been given us. We know merely the approximate dates that began and ended this period of his life. We know that he did get out of doors every now and then, walking to and from the nearest church. We do not know what trials and temptations came to sit at his bedside, or what consolations heaven may have sent him.

This is another of the mysteries in his life.

But it is absurdly easy to imagine him longing for his release, especially when reading the 119th Psalm, the first to come to his eye in the Little Hours, in his Office of the Blessed Virgin . . . "Woe is me that my sojourning is prolonged! I have dwelt with the inhabitants of Cedar; my soul hath been long a sojourner.

"With them that hated peace I was peaceful; when I spoke to them they fought against me without cause."

He was worn out, starved, frozen, loaded with chains, a bother to his sisters, a burden to his friends. Why didn't God call him home, or make him well? He had lived a long time with those who hated peace. And what had it got him? A few old splintered planks in a rusty old bed, a few rags of covers that never did keep out the cold, a few crusts of bread, a drink that a dog wouldn't touch, a solitude that repelled most of his friends, a wretched little room, a suit of clothes you could see through if you held it up to the light, and an overcoat he wore because it covered his bare knees from the world, not because there was any warmth in it. He didn't have anything at all, not even enough money to bury him.

Was this the way Jesus and Mary treated their slaves?

He must have reflected, in such hours of temptation, that Christ had left His own Mother behind Him, and bade her stay on the earth for many long years. She too felt the woe of a prolonged sojourning. She too knew the malice of them that hated peace.

Ah, many and many the time she must have wanted to see her Boy again, especially if it meant freeing herself from this valley of tears! But she knew there was a purpose in her staying here a while longer. A divine purpose. So it must have made her happy. Therefore it should make Matt happy too. What if he did feel useless, an incumbrance to his sisters and his friends, a prime nuisance even to himself? God's will be done.

It is absurdly easy to imagine temptations of another kind too, especially when Matt was beginning to feel well during the last springtime of his life. One can almost hear the tempter talking.

"Well, Matt, achree, there's life in the old boy yet, in spite of all your efforts to kill yourself, eh? What are you going to do with that life? It won't last long, you know. Are you going to die here in this dark rat hole, alone, neglected, ignored, totally forgotten? Your sister will come in some morning and find nothing but a grinning skull and a few silly bones — with those funny chains around them.

"Who wants to die chained to a bed, especially such a bed? Why don't you go out in a burst of glory, Matt me bucko,

since go out you must? You'll be getting your three pounds
odd again at Martins'; and you can make up, a little, for all
you've missed. Think of all you've gone without, Matt. You've
never smoked a cigarette, or even a good cigar. You've never
chewed tobacco. You've never stepped into a taxicab, an air-
plane, a balloon, or even a private motorcar. You've never read
a comic book, nor seen a peep show — or a movie. You've never
read a best seller. Mr. Proper Man Talbot. You've never played
a slot machine, nor have you danced to the music of a jazz band.

"You haven't taken advantage of a single modern invention,
and you haven't had a drink in more than forty years — except
that mixture you made up yourself!

"Why don't you have one last fling, Matt, before you kiss
the twentieth century good-by? Take a taxi to some tavern at
the beach. Nobody'll see you there. Take a friend with you,
if you like, someone who'll let you blow off steam the right
way. A pal, who'll even let you cry on her soft shoulders — cry
for all the nice things you've denied yourself these many years.
Give yourself one little break before you die, Matt.

"Remember how wonderful a pint of Guinness was, going
soft and cool-like down your gullet?

"Sure, who'll mind? Who'll scold you for the little pleasure,
Matt? The one who put those chains on you? On the contrary,
Matt. She'll understand. 'That's my boy,' she'll say. 'There's
no harm in him. Whatever he does is right.' You know how
mothers are, Matt, especially with sons they love, particularly
the sons who made themselves such willing slaves.

"Sure, Matt, 'tis the great saint you are, and you know it in
your heart. And saints have privileges not given the ordinary
man. And here's another thing, lad, that maybe you haven't
thought of. By going out this way — like a real he-man — you
can keep the secret of your holiness, as you've always wanted
to keep it. Take off your chains, man, get some decent clothes,
and have some real fun before it becomes too late."

Temptations come to every man, saint or sinner, slave of
Mary, or Saviour of the world. And many weird temptations
called on Matt Talbot, one can be sure. A man lying on his

back is more vulnerable than one kneeling upright in a bare room or a church. His mind isn't as keen, nor his will as sharp, nor his heart as well armored against the subtle fiends. But then our Lady, the chief Nurse of the Feeble, the Health of the Sick, the Refuge of Sinners, is always within call — with St. Michael at her command, and St. Raphael, and St. Gabriel, and all the other angels. And she watches her slaves vigilantly, lovingly, fiercely.

God permits the enemy to tempt some men even in the last moments of their lives, and to torment them more terribly than at any other moment — that the soul may win the greater glory with its triumph. It might have been that way with Matt.

Once he recovered enough of his old strength he began to relive his former routine. But on Sundays, at the advice of his doctor, he permitted himself a few indulgences.

If it were the first Sunday of the month he went to St. Francis Xavier's and received Communion with the Men's Sodality. The second Sunday found him in the Franciscan church across the river, receiving the Lord with his brothers of the Third Order. Other Sundays might place him with his Dominican brethren of the Living Rosary; or those of the Jesuit society of the Bona Mors, the good death; or with the people in the Pro-Cathedral where so many Masses were said at once.

He couldn't stay in any church, now, for all the Masses. He had to come home after the early Mass and feed his rebellious body, give it an hour or so of ease before he drove it out again to one of the late Masses.

He had to walk slowly; and often it felt good to stop for a moment and talk to some old friend. Undoubtedly, at such times, the ever curious headman of hell would come close enough to overhear what the two were saying, and to make a few more or less "sensible" suggestions.

"Now why don't the pair of you sit yourselves down in some cozy little snug and have a serious talk? You'll not be seeing poor Mickey again, Matt. Not in this life, nor the next. Ah, I don't have to tell you it's the saint you are, and you'll not even singe a hair of your holy head — few of them as you

125

have — in the flames of purgatory. But Mickey now, that's a different story. I have him tethered tighter to me than a certain Lady has yourself.

" 'Tis possible you might do the poor doomed soul a little good with your talk, Matt, and him with as dry a whistle on him as you had that day when no one would buy you a drop. Mickey himself contraried you that day, Matt. Have you forgotten? 'Twould be the grand thing now to buy him a pint in full forgiveness. And at the same time you could celebrate your approaching entrance into heaven.

"The grand throne that's waiting for you up there, Matt! And you not even thinking of buying a drink to celebrate your luck? Bedad, Matt, if you take poor Mickey here with you now over to the Widow Brown's you'll find some other friends there as hard up for the good word as Mickey himself. 'Tis Sunday, Matt, the day of rest. Rest yourself at the widow's with old friends, old brothers-in-lager, as it were, old drinking companions perishing for a friendly glass."

If the devil could approach him in front of a church and try to bar his way in; if the devil could make him walk for miles and miles about the city of Dublin looking for an altar rail he could approach, the devil could annoy him continually on his way home from church, even on the last day of his life.

Matt was feeling well early in the morning of that day, June 7, 1925. His sister, Mrs. Fylan, had visited him on Saturday evening, and felt quite hopeful for him. He had a good color. His eyes were bright and clear. And he talked in his old manner. She remarked that he looked splendid, and he told her, sitting on the edge of his bed, that he had never felt better in all his life, "thanks be to God."

His body may have looked healthy to his own eyes that night as he bathed it, but he didn't take off the chains. He must have seen they had become smooth, that they were embedded in his flesh, and that some of the links were rusted. He usually put on new chains when the rough iron had worn smooth and when the rust appeared. Perhaps he didn't feel quite strong enough yet to get out of the old chains and into the new. Perhaps some half-heard voice from heaven bade him let the chains alone.

It was the first Sunday of the month. Furthermore it was Trinity Sunday, one of the grandest feast days in all the calendar of grand feasts, the feast dedicated to paying honor and love and thanksgiving and adoration to Father, Son, and Holy Ghost.

Matt got up early, in the dark, and said long prayers. He rose from his knees some time after 5 o'clock, and shaved himself carefully. He went to early Mass at St. Francis Xavier's. He went to Communion with the Men's Sodality.

He didn't rush up to the Communion rail before Mass began, this morning, and leave his rusty iron pot of a hat below the extreme right end of the rail so that nobody would snatch his place and be first to receive Communion. The day of doing that sort of thing was far behind him. No, now he waited until it was time for the men in his pew to rise. He went with them, kneeling where he might.

He came home at the same slow pace, panting a little as he climbed the stairs. He ate. And then he reached for his prayer book and said his usual prayers. No one was there to see him and report. Not that particular morning. But Susan had been there many another Sunday. And it was always the same, she said. Always. Matt was a creature of habits.

There was one particular prayer he always said, when he came home after Mass. Nobody ever heard him say it aloud. But it isn't necessary to hear a prayer said to know it is familiar to a man. The evidence here is circumstantial, but irrefutable. The evidence is in the prayer book, for all the world to see. It is in the discoloration of certain pages. It is in the blacknesses made by Matt's sweating thumbs and fingers.

The blackest, the most worn, the most thumbed, the most read, and the most loved prayer of all, is this one that he must have said only after he came home from his early Masses:

O good Jesus, accept this Holy Communion as my viaticum, as if I were on this day to die. Grant that Thy most adorable Body and Blood may be the last remembrance of my soul;

the sacred names of Joseph, Mary, and Jesus my last words; my last affection an act of the purest, the most ardent love of Thee, and a sincere sorrow for my sins; my last consideration to expire in Thy divine arms, adorned with the gifts of Thy holy grace. Amen.

Matt put down the book, put on his hat, and started out to attend the 10 o'clock Mass at the Dominican church, the church of St. Saviour, not far away.

In the hallway he met his neighbor, John Mulvany.

"How are you, Mr. Talbot?" Mulvany said.

"A little weak, thank you," Matt said.

"Then maybe you ought to stay home. You went back to work too soon. That's what's the trouble."

"I felt all right last night," Matt insisted. "I felt all right until this morning."

He went upstairs, slowly, Mulvany noted. And he stayed upstairs a half an hour or so. Mulvany liked the little man. But he was curious about him too. There was something about Matt Talbot that — well, he didn't know — something holy, let's say.

There was a girl who had knocked at Mulvany's door one night, mistaking it for Matt's. She was out of a job and wanted help. But it wasn't money she wanted, it was prayers. Mulvany had shown her Matt Talbot's door and forgotten all about her. She came back a week or so later, so changed with happiness he didn't know her. He would have sworn it wasn't the same girl at all, at all, only she insisted she was. Matt wasn't in, that evening, so she bade Mulvany to tell the old man what a wonderful job his prayers had found for her. Yes, there was something about the little man — something odd, you might say, and kind of nice. Mulvany couldn't help watching him go up those wicked stairs. And he couldn't help shaking his head when he saw Matt come down again and start walking along the street.

The man should be in bed; but if he insisted on going to church, what could a neighbor do about it?

The city must have looked clean that Sunday (as it looked

128

to the visitor from America when he visited it twenty-seven years later). All the cabbage leaves that had yesterday littered the pavements around the stands of the market women, all the piles of rhubarb tops, and all the dust and dirt and muck in which the children had played so noisily, had disappeared. There was peace. There was sunshine. There was the odor of sweet green grass and of flowers. Maybe church bells were ringing, but a man who had lost his hearing on a wooden pillow would know nothing about that. People moved leisurely, softly, gracefully, going, like Matt, to worship Father, Son, and Holy Ghost, on this Their lovely day.

Along Mountjoy Square he went. Perhaps he had fleeting memories of women weeping and praying before the jail. Perhaps he was so filled with the glory of the day, and so confused with the weakness that had stealthily crept into his body, that he didn't remember anyone mourning there in the dust. He strolled along Gardiner Row, through Parnell Square, into Granby Row, and into the narrow thoroughfare that pitches, with a slight incline, down toward the rear of the great church — Granby Lane.

Halfway down the lane on the sidewalk the old man stopped, wavered, reached out an arm to get a purchase against the high wall, and fell.

It is possible that, in that last moment of his life, he saw the crossed pins in the cuff of his old coat. Dew and rain and fog and sleet and snow and time had discolored them. They didn't glint in the sun as they used to do. A man kept intending to change them, as he changed his fetters. But he forgot. A man tended to put off the little things, the easy things, but to do the difficult things as soon as possible — if only to have done with them.

It is possible the pin cross gleamed more brightly for Matt, in this farewell, than it ever had before. It is possible too, that he didn't see the cross in his sleeve, didn't need to see it. It is possible that he saw something else as he started to fall, and as his hand reached out to get a grip upon the wall. All we know is that he just dropped dead.

A woman ran to him. Her son came after her. They thought a glass of water might revive the fallen stranger. They carried him across the street to their shop, their home. But he slipped from their arms and lay still again. It was strange how light he was when they picked him up, and what weight had suddenly come on him. The boy raised his head, and the woman put the glass to the pale thin lips. But the man would never drink again.

Another man, coming from church, took a crucifix from his pocket, and hastily blessed the corpse. A Dominican priest, in his white habit, came running, summoned by an excited neighbor. He knelt above the wasted body and recited solemn words in Latin.

The Holy Trinity had heard Matt's oft-repeated prayer — "Accept this Holy Communion as my viaticum, as if I were to die today" . . . and had freed him forever from the trinity of evil, the world, the devil, and the flesh.

An ex-drunkard, drunk on love, was about to become a symbol of all that was opposed to a world drunk on hate and pride and power!

If he becomes the great saint of tomorrow it will be because he so humbly, and yet fiercely, fought all the evils of today — not because he once signed the pledge.

# 16

THE body lay in the wind and the dust, waiting the arrival of the ambulance — a small body neatly arranged at the side of the narrow lane that it might not interfere with traffic.

Every now and then an angel, with a twist of wind in his right hand would whip the overcoat open to give the world a look at the most singular pair of knees in all its history; every now and then, with his left hand, he would cover those knees reverently again.

Men and women, passing by on their way to or from Mass, blessed themselves, and said a prayer for the poor old man with the wonderful sweet look on his face, and him just after dropping dead. And they talked about him as they hurried away.

"Did you see the overcoat of him now? Whisht! If the post office clark gave you a twopenny stamp that thin you'd be calling him names wouldn't be carved on his tombstone. Sure it must have been Noah himself had that coat when it was new — or did Noah get it from his father now, or his grand-

131

father? The coat died long before the poor dear man that wore it. Thank God it's not bitter cold, the day."

"And the pins. Did ye see the two pins he'd saved, the thrifty old spalpeen? Sure 'tis easy to tell he'll not be a married man, with them bent old black pins showing in his sleeve."

Nobody knew the pins were a glorious standard, a battle flag valiantly carried through forty-one years of prayer and penance. Nobody realized that they were a fitting symbol of the great day they celebrated. Since it was a memory of Christ — that symbol — and since Christ was God, and God was a Triune God, the pins had reminded Matt not only of the Redeemer of the world, but also of Father, Son, and Holy Ghost. And of our Lady, the Virgin Mother standing at the foot of the cross, the special darling of each person of the Holy Trinity.

It was a bit of a miser lay there, some thought, and him saving two pins like that, and never using them. It was something of a joke, they said, him saving pins for his old age. The words themselves were the beginning of a joke, wouldn't you say now? "For two pins I'd do this"; "for two pins I'd do that." He was a beggar. He was a tramp. He was a roustabout, an old drunk as likely as not, fallen because he had too much drink — free drinks of course, for there wouldn't be enough silver on the likes of him decently to wet a toper's two dry tonsils.

Nobody knew he was a soldier of the cross, with knightly armor tight against his flesh. Nobody knew he was a courtier and a lover and a slave of the loveliest Queen God ever made. Nobody suspected he might, some day, be enrolled among the greatests of the saints.

The ambulance came, and took the body away. Sometime later, Sister Ignatius of the Sisters of Mercy, was assigned to prepare it for burial. It had not yet been identified. The hospital authorities weren't sure it would ever be identified. But that didn't matter very much, did it? The little old man looked like a corpse that would never be missed. It would take money to bury it in consecrated ground. And who was to pay money for such as him?

Sister Ignatius attacked his clothes with her scissors. Christ's garments had been worth at least three shakes of the dice. But this man's? Nobody would throw dice for these clothes.

There was a prayer stirring in the good nun's mind. Therefore her mind wasn't exactly on her work. It was a prayer almost as old as the human race. It was the prayer of a man named Job.

"Who will grant me that my words may be written? Who will grant me that they may be marked down in a book with an iron pen and in a plate of lead, or be graven with an instrument on the flint stone?"

If all the words weren't there as she ripped up the cloth with the shears, and in their proper order, the meaning was present.

"For I know that my Redeemer liveth and in the last day I shall rise out of the earth, and I shall be clothed again with my skin, and in my flesh I shall see God, my Saviour!"

There was a prayer too, in her heart, for the soul that had left the body on this feast day of the Trinity.

So, at first, she didn't know what to make of the sound of steel biting into iron. Nor did she know what to make of the shock of the scissors stopping dead in their work and refusing to go on.

Chains, she saw, then. Chains!

The sound of the scissors on the link of the dead man's chain echoed and re-echoed around the world. But it didn't seem to be the same sound. It became more like the noise a shovel makes when it is plunged into gold-bearing gravel.

Sister Ignatius had struck gold, holy people said to one another. Sister had thrust a shovel into a strange cold clay and found a nugget, a veritable saint of God! Ah, but a strange saint. A layman. An ordinary worker. A man in overalls. A fellow that worked in a lumberyard and had callouses on his hands and slivers in his fingers. A man that wore chains on his

**133**

body, and pieces of old rope. Listen to the official report, man. This is what they found on him when they got him to the morgue:

"Around the middle of his waist were two chains and a knotted rope. One chain we took to be an ordinary chain used as a horse trace, and the other a little thinner. Both were entwined by a knotted rope and medals were attached to the chain by cords. Both were deeply embedded in the flesh and rusted. Also on the left arm was found a light chain tightly wound above the elbow, and on the right arm above the elbow a knotted cord. On his left leg a chain was bound round with a cord below the knee, and on the right leg, in the same position, was some heavy knotted cord. Around his neck was a very big beads and attached to same were a great many religious medals. Some of the medals were as big as a half crown and others ordinary sodality medals."

Sister Ignatius blessed herself. These chains might be a sort of religious habit too, and as pleasing to God and His Mother as her own habit, or the habit of any monk. A religious habit for a layman? Indeed that's what these rusty chains might be. For weren't they Mary's own chains the man had fastened on himself?

Glory be to God, could this poor body be the body of a saint?

All over the world people talked about the "gold strike." All over the world people talked of other holy laymen. Dominic Savio, now, that St. John Bosco wrote about, the fifteen-year-old boy that would some day, please God, wear a full-sized halo. And Maria Goretti, the virgin and martyr who would also be raised to the altar by some pope; God bless her, she was only a child of ten or eleven. And wasn't there a man named Labre, a tramp or something, waiting on the patience of the cardinals and the pope for recognition?

One, two, three. And this Talbot — it's possible he might be number four. And then there was St. Rose of Lima, and St. Catherine of Siena, and a few more. Only a handful of lay people; barring the martyrs. But then a man could spend his life counting, and live to be a hundred, and never count all the lay martyrs.

Only a handful — barring the martyrs — but maybe it was just beginning, the lay saints were.

Where did the man get the idea of the chains? From *True Devotion* was it? And what was True Devotion? And who was St. Louis Marie de Montfort who gave that True Devotion to lay people?

The chains that had freed Matt Talbot from the world had attached the world to him. The vein of pure gold they had uncovered through their collision with the blades of a Sister's scissors had started a spiritual gold rush in every part of the world.

Men and women began to read about St. Louis Marie, the sainted slave of Mary, and the prophecy he had made:

> The power of Mary over all the devils will break out especially in latter times. . . . Her humble slaves and her poor children . . . she will raise up to make war. . . . They shall be little and poor in the world's esteem, and abased before all . . . they shall be rich in grace . . . great and exalted before God in sanctity, superior to all creatures by their animated zeal . . . in union with Mary, they shall crush the head of the devil and cause Jesus Christ to triumph.

The gold of the lay apostolate — that's what those chain-struck scissors had exposed! If you could find one nugget there, you could find millions of others!

The pope was calling to the laity with anxious and loving words, asking them to take part in the restoration of the world to Christ, begging them to take an active part.

The lay apostolate! Catholic action! These were new words. They were new to bishops and to priests. They were amazingly and gloriously new to ordinary lay men and women.

Already there was one lay apostolate practicing Catholic Action. That was the Legion of Mary. It had been started in Dublin, in 1921, among a group of people imbued with True Devotion, among a handful of lay people wearing chains as symbols of their slavery to Christ and Mary.

Had Matt Talbot anything to do with that?

When the body was identified, Matt's Franciscan brothers put the brown habit of St. Francis on it. The Men's Sodality of St. Francis Xavier's furnished the coffin and paid for the burial. The chains, the ropes, and the medals were buried with the body, on June 11, the feast of Corpus Christi — the feast of the Body of Christ.

A wooden marker was placed upon the grave by someone who wanted to visit the place again. Glasnevin is a huge cemetery. There are many paths in it. A visitor can easily get lost. And if there is no sign to say who lies beneath this plot, and who beneath the sod beyond, a visitor will never find the grave he seeks. The grave of Matt's mother was lost that way; and also the grave of his father.

Eventually, through the efforts and contributions of Raphael O'Callaghan and other friends, a beautiful Celtic cross was erected at the head of the mound. And the image of the Sacred Heart was graven in the cross.

That cross has served as the cornerstone for many a "lay apostolic Catholic action" group.

Much more than grass has sprouted from the soil in which the little slave was put to rest on the feast day of Christ's Body.

# Part III

# The Words of a Papal Decree

"Ireland has deserved for many centuries to be called the island of Saints and the nurse of Heroes.

"This Congregation is now considering, with the hope of a probable happy result, the Cause of the workman, Matt Talbot.

"May God grant that the example of this Servant of God may preserve workmen from the teachings of those who are trying to upset the social order. . . .

"After only six years in the Dublin Curia, the Informative Process was begun concerning the report of his sanctity. . . . Meanwhile many letters were sent to the Supreme Pontiff by all the archbishops and bishops of Ireland, by the President of the Nation, by the Apostolic Nuncio, by many abbots, by the provincial superiors of many orders and congregations, by the Lord Mayor of Dublin, by the Trade Unions, and by others, asking for the Introduction of his Cause.

"A full report having been made to His Holiness Our Lord Pope Pius XII, on the twenty-eighth day of February, 1947, His Holiness, agreeing with the Rescript of the Eminent Cardinals, deigned to sign with his own hand the commission for the Introduction of the Cause of the Servant of God, Matthew Talbot."

(*From an English translation of the papal decree posted on the doors of churches in Ireland.*)

# 17

MEN walked softly through Matt's room in the days that followed, looking for clues to his sanctity, men he never knew. Some looked at the books on the chair, on the bed, in a great box on the floor, wondering at their number, their quality, the spirituality and knowledge compressed between their covers.

"Could he have understood all these?" one would ask another, looking at names such as Blosius, Newman, Père Grou, L'Abbé Sertillange, Père Eymard, and Mary of Agreda.

Another would look at passages Matt had underlined, or at excerpts he had made from pages that enthralled or delighted him. There were notes everywhere, badly written words scrawled on pieces of rough wastepaper. Surely the key to the man's personality lay in these notes?

"Listen to this, Father," a layman would say. "This sums up the man himself. 'The kingdom of heaven was promised not to the sensible and the educated but to such as have the spirit of little children.' "

Some read aloud, many times, the prayer Matt had framed and hung on the wall below the crucifix:

I adore Thee, O most sweet Saviour, Jesus, expiring on the cross for our sake. I have no words to express my gratitude for the infinite Goodness Thou hast evinced in dying to redeem me. O Eternal Father, I offer Thee Thy dear Son who hung on the tree of the cross, naked, torn, pierced with thorns and nails, bleeding, anguishing, suffering, expiring. Yes, my God, it is Thine own and only begotten Son I offer to Thee in this lamentable condition; receive His divine sacrifice, accept this offering that I make Thee. It is my ransom. It is the Blood of God; it is God Himself that I offer Thee now, for the payment and acquittal of my debts. I offer Him also for the relief of the Souls in Purgatory, of the sick, the poor and the afflicted, the grace of a happy death for the agonizing, the conversion of sinners, the perseverance of the just, and to impetrate for myself and for those specially dear to me the grace of dying in Thy friendship and love, also the grant of their present urgent petitions. Amen. May the most holy and adorable will of God be ever accomplished in all things. May it be praised forever and ever. Amen.

"Impetrate," some said after attentively reading the prayer Matt had read every day. "What does that mean — to impetrate? To beg? To implore? To obtain? Who's got a dictionary?"

It wasn't only Matt who needed to look up words.

Men touched the wooden planks on which Matt had slept, and the pillow that had rested and deafened his head, and the table at which he had read, and eaten, and talked to Christ and Mary. And every last man of them, according to neighbors, knelt and said a prayer before he took a last look around the dreary but wonderful room and clumped his way down to the street.

Raphael O'Callaghan, who had come — perhaps to recover the books he had let Matt borrow — brought there his friend, Sir Joseph Glynn. He suggested Sir Joseph write a book about Matt Talbot.

"Who is he?" Sir Joseph asked. "Somebody important?"

O'Callaghan told him about Matt, promised to introduce him to people who had known the little man, and to see that he obtained all the material he needed for a story.

O'Callaghan meant well, but he didn't know what a task he was giving the biographer. The only three people who could give any writer the real story of this candidate for sainthood had long since died. His mother. His spiritual director. His intimate friend, Msgr. Hickey.

There were people who remembered the Monsignor when he was the president of Clonliffe College. The Monsignor had told one of them a few incidents about Matt Talbot, and had added:

"Whenever I wanted a particular favor from heaven I asked Matt to pray for it. His prayers were never refused."

Sir Joseph interviewed Matt's sisters. They had never known their brother well, they confessed, had never shared his complete confidence. They were in awe of him, and seldom said anything to him beyond . . . "How are you today, Matt?" . . . "Has the cat got your tongue?" . . . "Is there anything I can do for you?" . . . "You're looking well," . . . "You look like a death's head, Matt, and it sitting on shoulders thin enough to shave yourself with; 'tis a wonder it don't fall off." . . . "Why don't you take a little care of yourself?" . . . or "How much is it today you'll be sending to the missions?"

They had heard a few things from their mother. But that was long ago, and hard to believe. They knew nothing about Matt's wearing chains, though they had seen chains in his room. They had never asked him about such things. One didn't ask Matt too many questions. And sure, it's true as truth itself, if the poor fellow had died at home they'd never have let a single solitary soul on earth hear a whisper about those chains.

Not a whisper, Sir Joseph!

Not even the hint of a whisper.

It was the providence of God that he died as he did, and let the world find out what sort of man he was.

Sir Joseph talked to Matt's friends and employers. They

couldn't tell him much. They could furnish only a few bones of the skeleton the biographer sought in the earth of their memories. Not one of them had had the least suspicion that there was anything approaching sanctity in Matt. Oh, of course, they knew he went to daily Mass and Communion. But many people did that. They knew he was "kind of finicky" about his food; but it hadn't occurred to many that he fasted every day, especially in Lent, and during June, the month of the Sacred Heart. They had never heard of his nightly vigils, his elaborate schedule of prayers and devotions, his austere penances. Matt sleep on boards? It was news to them, astounding news. Matt use a log for a pillow? He had never mentioned it to anyone.

Some remembered "queer things," now that Sir Joseph brought them to mind. Like the time Ed Carew's wife was sick, and Matt promised to pray for her. He told Ed not to worry, the woman would be all right. She did recover too. And another time Ed asked Matt to pray for a brother-in-law. Matt said he would, but advised Ed to be reconciled to God's will if the man should die. Sure enough, he died.

There were many stories like that, but nothing to indicate Matt had ever worked miracles through prayer. A man in a Dublin hospital, for instance, begged God for help. He was an alcoholic and knew he could not help himself. A nurse had him kneel and pray for Matt Talbot's canonization. He did it, just to please the nurse. But he got up quickly, and cried out, "I'm cured."

Sir Joseph worked hard to dig out all there was. But Matt had buried himself deeply and well. It was only in the room he left behind him, that Sir Joseph got any real indication of Matt's greatness. He got this from the saints that had inhabited the place with Matt. Matt had invited them there, and had kept them there as permanent guests. They could be seen in pictures, in books, in the scraps of paper that littered the room.

The Evangelists. The Apostles. The great penitents such as Mary of Magdala, Mary of Egypt, Augustine, Ignatius, Paul, and the good thief on the cross. Matt loved them well. He loved others too.

He loved the virgins and martyrs, the founders of religious orders, the mystics, the lay saints, men and women such as King Louis of France, King Edward of England, Queen Elizabeth of Hungary, St. Veronica, St. Monica, St. Catherine of Siena. He loved the Jesuits, the Franciscans, the Dominicans, the Redemptorists, the Cistercians. He loved the doctors of the Church, read them many times and quoted often from them. He loved St. Ambrose especially, and St. Francis de Sales, and — perhaps above all — he loved St. Louis Marie de Montfort, the Little Flower, St. Patrick, and St. Bride.

Sir Joseph wrote, at first, only a thin pamphlet about Matt Talbot. Within a week ten thousand copies had been sold. Within a few months the sales had topped the hundred thousand mark. Later the author enlarged the book, adding new facts he had learned, and reproducing some of the notes Matt had left behind him. This became the source book for all other biographers.

"These little scraps of paper," Sir Joseph wrote, "reveal the very soul of the man and show his own beautiful character much better than the words of a biographer can do. They shall be allowed to tell their own tale."

What can another biographer do but help himself to them, for the sake of his readers, and thank Sir Joseph for the labor he had compiling them? Here they are:

"Speak not evil of the rich man in the private chamber because even the birds of the air will carry thy voice and he that hath wings will tell what thou hast said. Book Cle. & C 19 V.

"Cursed be the deceitful man, says God, who has a male in his flock and yet sacrifices an infirm creature to Me, because I am a great King says the Lord of Hosts and My name is terrible among the nations. The prophet Malachy the 1. C. & 14 V.

"Draw me after Thee oh Heart of Jesus and I shall run in the odor of the ointments.

"Grant me oh Jesus Thy Grace and Love and I shall be rich enough.

"The sparrow has found herself a house and the turtle dove a nest to deposit her young. Thy heart oh Jesus shall be my rest and repose.

"May my eyes and my heart be always on the wound of Thy Blessed Heart oh Jesus.

"Who shall separate us from the Heart of Jesus.

"Heart of Jesus be Thou the object of all the affections of my heart.

"Lord give me of that water flowing from Thy Heart and I shall never thirst.

"Heart of Jesus support the weak, clothe me with Thy strength.

"St. Veronica — The Blessed told her to banish all anxiety for her to 3 letters — The 1st — Purity of the affections by placing her whole heart in God alone, loving no creature but in Him, and for her, 2nd — Never to murmur or be impatient at the sins or any behaviour of others but to bear them with interior peace and patience and humbly to pray for them, and 3rd — to set apart some time every day to meditate on the Passion of Christ.

"Liberty of Spirit means that freedom from self-love that makes the soul prompt in doing God's will in the least thing.

"O most sweet Jesus mortify within me all that is bad — make it die. Put to death in me all that is vicious and unruly. Kill whatever displeases Thee, mortify within me all that is my own. Give me true humility, true patience and true charity. Grant me the perfect control of my tongue, my —

"What is Mystical Theology . . . (It) is the science that deals with God and divine things; the truths revealed by God and all that results from revelations. The word mystical means secret, hidden, obscure. Mystical Theology, therefore, is that part of the General Science of Theology which treats about the secret and hidden things. Union of the soul with God, it is also used in the present treatise C. the 12 to denote . . .

"When Our Lord showed Sister Francesca of the Bleeding

144

[*sic*] Sacrament, a Spanish Carmelitess, the loss of a soul and several times in a vision compelled her positively to study separate tortures of that place, (He) upbraided her for weeping. Francesca why weepest thou? She fell prostrate at the Sacred Feet and said Lord for the damnation of that soul and the manner in which it has been damned. He vouchsafed to reply, Daughter it hath chosen to damn itself I have given it many helps of grace that it might be saved.

"As to nobility of blood, true nobility is to be derived only from the blood of the Son of God.

"Love is a Sweet Tyrant, sweet to the person beloved but a tyrant to the lover that is Jesus Christ that is God.

"The heathen philosophers, when (they) knew God, had not glorified Him as God or given thanks; but became vain in their thoughts; and their foolish hearts were darkened; wherefore God gave them up to the shameful affections and to the desire of their own heart to uncleanness."

(Sir Joseph explains that he had altered this note as it was "slightly mixed up through misplacing some of the words." It may be explained here that a subsequent hand has punctuated the lines to make their meaning unmistakable.)

"He that oppresseth the poor upbraideth his maker, but he that hath pity on the poor honoureth him. Prov. 14 C. 13 V.

"God, says St. Augustine, can only be honoured by love.

"How I long that Thou mayest be master of my heart my Lord Jesus.

"O King of Penitents who pass for fools in the opinion of the world but very dear to You, oh Jesus Christ.

"The exterior acts of religion are 3 — Adoration, Sacrifice, and Vows.

"Three Substances were united in Christ — His Divinity, His Soul, and His Body.

"Absolute miracle is from God alone, a miracle from an angel is an efficient miracle done by His own strength. Hume tells us that a miracle may be accurately defined a transgression of a law of nature by a particular volition of the Deity.

"Should (you) ask me what is Grace, I answer you Grace

**145**

as Divines define it is a participation of the Divine nature that is God, Sanctity, Purity, and Greatness by virtue of which a man rises from the baseness and filth he received from Adam.

"The prophet Amos C. 8 v.9 & 10. The sun shall go down at midday and I will make the earth dark in the day of Light and I will turn your feasts into mourning and all songs into lamentations.

"All flesh have sinned and all flesh must suffer. St. Ambrose says without combat there is no victory and without victory there is no crown.

"Our Lord appeared to St. Gertrude pale, weary and bleeding and dirt stained and said open your heart my daughter for I want to go in and lie down. I am weary of these days of sin.

"Sin is an excessive evil because it is an infinite evil.

"Perfect happiness consists of the full activity of a perfect nature. The angels have it.

"At present the human body is an animal body inasmuch as to preserve its life on this earth so it is (essential) to nourish it with earthly food.

"Jesus, says Origen, is the Sun of Justice arising with the Spring of Grace upon our hearts.

"The Heart of Jesus is with me. Stop. Cease. The inhabitants of Antioch it is related once arrested a violent earthquake by writing on doors of their houses Jesus Christ is with us, Cease.

"Sir Henry Wotton a great authority on the point, Ambassador at Venice, tells us that an Ambassador is one sent to foreign Courts to invent lies for his country's good.

"O Blessed Mother obtain from Jesus a share of His folly.

"It is the will of God that man should have two lives, the one natural and the other supernatural.

"The sons of Man neither know what is the greatness of what is eternal nor the baseness of what is temporal. The time of life is but a career of death in which no man is permitted to make stay.

"The Pope is subject to no human authority. This is his

temporal power. Christ is not divided, so neither is His Church divided. After all the world can do God is still upon His Throne. The obedience of Jesus Christ to the will of God was the recognition of the Sovereignty of God over the will of Man.

"The teaching of theologians (is) that all venial sins with which a just man dies are remitted as to the guilt at the moment when the soul is separated from the body, by virtue of an Act of Love of God and the perfect contrition which it then excites over all its faults. In fact the soul at this moment knows its condition perfectly, and the sins of which it has been guilty before God, and all the stain of guilt has then disappeared but the pain remains to be endured in all its rigour and long duration.

"To constitute a mortal sin three circumstances must be united — 1 — The matter must be grave and 2 — the mind must have a full knowledge of the culpability of the act which it commits or of the omission which it permits or of the danger of the occasion of sin to which it exposes itself 3 — the will must decide with an entire consent and a criminal preference for the forbidden act, the culpable omission, or the dangerous occasion.

"The Body and the Soul of Jesus Christ were united by the hypostatic Union, that is by the personal assumption of our manhood into God to the Person of the eternal Son, two natures in one person, Jesus Christ . . . The use of the will is to do good but the abuse of the will is to do evil.

"One Our Father, one Hail Mary in honour of (the) life ignominy of Jesus . . . offer yourself to God with Joy and Peace. Man enjoys by the Union of God to his nature an advantage which the angels never possessed.

"The Kingdom of Heaven was promised not to the sensible and the educated but to such as have the spirit of little children.

"Oh Virgin I only ask three things — the Grace of God, the Presence of God, the Benediction of God.

"In Meditation we labour to seek God, by reasoning and

by good acts, but in Contemplation we behold Him, without labour, already found. In Meditation the mind labours, operates with its power, but in Contemplation it is God Himself who operates, and the soul merely receives the infused gifts.

"What do I want to speak to you when I have Jesus to speak to me?"

Perhaps, in that last note, Matt was rebuking himself.

# 18

EVENTUALLY Sir Joseph's little book was translated into more than a score of languages, and was distributed over many parts of the world. Copies came even to America. And one, by a happy chance, fell into the hands of a tired old newspaperman with plenty of time to read, and to think.

He digested the facts the Englishman had gathered and presented. But he was not overly impressed. The author had done a workmanlike job. But he had not loved his subject, merely admired him. He had not given him rebirth. It takes love to make the dead live in the hearts of living men and women. Love, more than skill.

Only after he had refreshed himself with the honey Matt had extracted from so many wise and loving hearts — and which he had left to his heirs and assigns — did the newspaperman begin to see the Irish candidate for sainthood with any clarity of vision. Only then did he begin to appreciate the man.

He read the dry facts again, lit them with his imagination

and his growing love, and set them blazing into something like a resurrection.

Oddly enough this resurrection, this re-creation, this re-animation, or reincarnation — call it what you will — began with Matt's death and progressed backward toward his school days. It began with the vision of an old derby falling from a bald head and rolling back and forth in drunken semicircles on a dirty street, teetering on its worn rim. That hat had more life in it than the man who had worn it so many years. The wind blew it away. The wind blew bits of paper down the lane, millions of bits of paper. They made a screen that hid the body and the people gathering around it. The newspaperman could read words on some of those pieces of paper. "Jesus . . . Mary . . . Mother . . . Christ . . . St. Gertrude . . . St. Vincent . . . St. Ignatius . . . Kingdom of Heaven." And he could smell a sweet odor in the wind that blew them. Some fell on his lips, and the taste was sweet.

The sun was shining on the twisting, turning, dancing scraps of paper; and they twinkled and gleamed and glistened as though they had been cut from the stars in the milky way. They reminded the reporter of "Slim" Lindbergh, "the flying fool," when he became the hero of heroes to all the boys in the world. They recalled the frenzied joy in Washington, D. C., the gathering of the nation's great, the happy and excited crowds who came to greet the immortal flyer, the parade — the ranks of soldiers moving in perfect step down the wide clean avenue, rifles held just so, bayonets meticulously aligned and glinting — all the toy soldiers a boy had dreamed of in the long ago, come suddenly alive to do him honor, even as Matt Talbot was coming alive to greet a dreamer. Then there was that fantastic reception in New York, with Lindy riding in an open car up the canyon of Broadway, and millions and millions of scraps of paper flying down from the windows of the skyscrapers along the way.

God and Mary and all the saints and angels, it seemed to the reporter, might have welcomed Matt to heaven with more tons of shining confetti than had honored Lindbergh. And the confetti was made of his own love letters!

Odd material for God to bother with? Perhaps. They were atrociously written. The spelling was bad. The words were often misplaced. Sometimes words were left out of sentences. Some sentences were never finished. Some sentences did not make sense. But love had written all those words to Love; and Love would repay a hundred thousandfold. The wind that swept down Granby Lane had sent those love words flying over all the earth.

And how the earth needed them! And how it needed Matt!

Truly, God raises up saints in each age for His own purposes. This was an age of indulgence, of luxury, softness, comfort, ease — ease of body, ease of morals, ease of principles, ease of almost everything but conscience. This was an age that needed the example of such a man as Matthew Talbot!

The paper snowstorm passed from the reporter's vision. The body had disappeared. The street itself had dissolved into nothingness. The attempt at resurrection had failed dismally; and it would not be repeated.

There were other pamphlets the reporter read, but they were mostly rewrites of Sir Joseph's story. There was no power in them, no warmth, no fruitfulness. Must Matt Talbot, then, stay dead?

In 1947, Father Albert H. Dolan, a Carmelite priest who had written a pamphlet about the Dublin hermit, went to Ireland with Fr. Ronald F. Gray, to make a further study of Matt's life, and to bring back all the relics possible to obtain. The Carmelites had begun the "Matt Talbot Legion," with the aim of aiding alcoholics through "prayer and education." They wanted to display the relics in their Englewood, New Jersey, headquarters, to excite devotion to Matt.

Father Dolan brought the relics back; but he did not bring Matt with them.

The reporter felt that if he were ever to know the strange little man he must go to Dublin and get acquainted with him.

And where should he start to seek him? He felt he must begin in Granby Lane.

The street was narrower than he had thought, and shorter in length. It had a sidewalk on its left, obeying the British traffic law, "keep left." There was a bar at its beginning; dance halls and brewery storage rooms, a Catholic mission, and tenement flats in its middle; and tombstone-cutting yards in its ending. It was but a block long. It led one to the back of the Dominican church, then turned abruptly, became another street, and went on, untroubled, about its daily business.

The reporter half expected to see a dusty old derby rolling drunkenly on the pavement. He was almost disappointed that it wasn't there.

Halfway down the lane, on the right, there was a shrine. It was just a box or stand or table, fitted snugly against the bricks of a narrow wall. There were flowers in vases on the top of the stand, and vases of flowers above them, on either side of a plaque. High over all was a small Celtic cross in its own homemade box.

Everything was clean. The wood of the stand, and of the prie-dieu someone had placed before it, had been recently dusted. The bricks in back of it — the wall that rose between the door of a flat building and the wider door of a stable or warehouse or barn or yard — had been painted a glossy black. The flowers, clusters of iris and lupines, were fresh and gay. The plaque was spotless.

A thin man with thick eyeglasses was kneeling before the shrine, a heavy Rosary in his hands. A black umbrella, its crooked handle tipped with yellow metal, lay beside him.

Across the lane, almost directly opposite the kneeling man, a large crucifix had been affixed to the wall, high above the sidewalk.

Looking across the shoulder of the man on his knees, the visitor read the plaque. "This is the place where Matt Talbot died. June 7, 1925. R.I.P."

The crucifix appeared to deny the exactness of those words.

It was on that side of the lane, it seemed to insist, that Matt had fallen dead.

The man at the shrine got up, that the visitor might have the privilege of kneeling.

"American," he said, picking up his umbrella. It was not a question. It was a label.

"Yes."

"You'd not see the like of this anywhere in your part of the world," the other said. He looked three times as tall, standing, as he had kneeling. "A shrine against a wall, and someone kneeling there with the beads — you'd sooner see a three-headed calf than such a strange sight in Chicago or New York. But don't let me disturb you."

"Did you know Matt?"

"I did not, God be good to me. But it's a lot of Matt Talbots you'll find in Dublin. Odd creatures leading lives of dreadful poverty, frightful penances, and tremendous sanctity. It's not every one of them, though, you'd find kneeling outside any church with only a light overcoat against the wind. It gets bitter cold here in winter and colder than that to a body that's had only a few hours' sleep and nothing but a few bites to eat."

"Was it here he died," the newspaperman asked, motioning toward the shrine, "or there?"

The man nodded in the direction of the crucifix.

"He fell dead on the sidewalk, some maintain. Others say he died after he was carried across the lane. Somebody was so sure it was under the crucifix Matt breathed his last that he came in the middle of the night, with chisel and hammer and burlap bag. He cut a great chunk of cement out of the sidewalk, and carried it away. Of course the crucifix wasn't there in Matt's day. It was put up years later, as a marker."

He smiled wryly, and shook his head. "You can believe the plaque," he said, "or you can take the word of the cross. Let you not fight about which side of the street he died on. Let you be satisfied to know he died in this lane. Sure, the whole street is a shrine, barroom, dance halls, ale kegs, and all.

**153**

It's one of the shortest streets in the world, but one of the best known. Let you not quarrel about just which spot in it is the holiest. Good day, and God be with you."

A woman with two little boys came up the lane, from the direction of the church, while the visitor made use of the prie-dieu.

As she came abreast of the crucifix she stood on tiptoe and kissed the feet. The older of the two boys — he was about five — asked to kiss it too. She lifted him up. He was a heavy child and it was all the woman could do to hold him. When she lowered him she raised the baby to the cross. The infant kissed the wood, with a loud moist smack, as though it had become a custom. His brother cried. He wanted to kiss the feet again. His mother frowned, sighed, made a gesture of resignation, then gathered her forces together, and lifted him the second time.

"He's a greedy one for Christ, God bless him," the mother said, settling the baby in the small cart he fitted so snugly, "but he's getting so heavy I don't know what to do."

She ignored the shrine.

# 19

"AH, ANOTHER of the Magi come to do reverence at the grave of Matt Talbot!" Henry O'Mara greeted the visitor. "Another wise man led across the sea by the splendor of a star."

Mr. O'Mara is the editor of *Vexilla Regis,* the Maynooth Laymen's annual, and the chief superintendent of the Dublin police. He was with Father Senan, O.F.M.Cap., editor of the *Capuchin Annual,* which is as well known in America as it is in Ireland, the author of a number of books, and one of the most respected art critics in the Emerald Isle. The two were in the priest's tiny and crowded office.

"Don't class me with the Magi," the newspaperman said. "Put me down as one who would like to know what Matt was like when he was on his knees and not in his cups, and who would like to introduce him to Canada and the United States."

"What you'd see in Matt's face," the priest said, "would be a reflection of the forgiving, kindly, heartening face of Christ. And the beautiful face of Mary. And the faces of saints and angels. Never forget the angels, for they constantly

**155**

look upon the glory of God. Can you show all that to the people of America?"

The reporter wasn't at all confident he could. "Can you show it to the people of Dublin, Father?" he demanded.

"We try to," Father Senan answered. "But there are many in this city, and this country, who don't have to be urged to seek for the face of God, who know it well.

"Your Alcoholics Anonymous, now, must have a glimmer of what Matt saw, or else they could not have devised such a spiritual platform. Nor could they have grown so rapidly, and to such numbers. 'See how these alcoholics love one another,' a man might say. If you could give those people a clear picture of Matt, you'd help them grow still bigger; and you'd help your country in other ways. But Matt was more than just an ex-drinker."

The priest opened a drawer of his big desk and stirred his hand blindly among an assortment of papers. "Speaking of the Magi," he said, "I thought you might like to have this picture that was found in Matt's room." It was a picture of the Magi, cut out of a magazine or book.

"And this one too," the priest added, producing a picture of Jacob who, posing as his brother Esau, was presenting a dish to his blind father. Rebecca, the mother, was shown outside the door of the tent.

The newspaperman, thinking of St. Louis Marie, managed to say thanks. What, exactly, was it the saint had said that fitted so perfectly the meaning of this second picture? It was not until he had opened the book on True Devotion that he found the passage:

Rebecca made Jacob come near to his father's bed. The good man touched him, embraced him, and even kissed him with joy, being content and satisfied with the well-dressed viands which he had brought him; and having smelt with much contentment the exquisite perfume of his garments he cried out ... "the odor of my son ... is like the odor of a full field that the Lord hath blest." This odor of the full field which charms the heart of the Father is nothing else than the odor of the

156

virtues and merits of Mary, who is a field full of grace, where God the Father has sown His only Son, as a grain of the wheat of the elect. O, how a child, perfumed with the good odor of Mary, is welcome with Jesus Christ, who is the Father of the world to come! O how promptly and how perfectly is such a child united to his Lord!

Matt must have read that passage too, gazing at the picture of Jacob. And he, or one of his friends, had drawn heavy pencil marks around the kneeling Jacob. If one looks at the picture from the reverse side he sees what appears to be the outline of an angel.

The American saw that Father Senan had a scissors in his hand. He wondered if it were the one that had struck a spark from Matt Talbot's chain. But it was only an editor's shears, and the priest was merely using it, not exhibiting it. He was cutting a piece of paper in two.

"Matt wrote on both sides of this," he said. "Which half do you want?"

"The top half," the visitor answered, trying to appear as calm as though nobody had offered him a great treasure.

"You may be disappointed," Father Senan said. "Matt was interested in history too, it seems, as well as in religion. And in statistics. He was a better-read man than anybody realizes."

The reporter studied one side of the paper in his hand. "Balthazar Gerard who shot the william of nassau Prince of orange he was 28 years old. he was 6½ years waicthing (waiting? or watching?) him his mother was from Besancon."

"William the Silent," Count of Nassau and Prince of Orange, had turned from the Catholic Church because of the persecution of Lutherans and Calvinists ordered by King Philip II of Spain, the self-righteous, self-appointed, bloody "champion" of the religion of Love. He had left the Church and become a Calvinist that he might fight with his people against tyranny and oppression, and help them enjoy what he considered the right of every man, liberty of conscience. Philip had offered a reward for his murder. Balthazar Gerard, a Burgundian and

**157**

presumably a Catholic, collected this blood money when h shot the prince at Delft, on July 9, 1584.

Why was Matt interested in this old crime? Was he mourning over the dead prince? Was he praying for his soul? Was he also praying for the assassin, and for the king who spurred him on?

How often has the Church been betrayed by its own! How often has some mad monarch or prelate tried to teach religion with fire and famine and sword — the crayons the devil uses to make his own mark on the blackboard of the world!

How many sermons were hidden in those few lines, how much philosophy, how many prayers?

The words were traced with two pencils, one with a purple lead, the other with a blue one. The words on the opposite side of the paper were written with a black lead. And the handwriting, at first glance, seemed entirely different. There must have been a number of years between the day Matt filled the first side, and the day he turned the paper over and availed himself of the blank space it afforded.

"Catacombs," this side begins, "there is 900 miles of Galleries and 7 millions of Graves] in year 1846 there were 130,000 Couples Married in England 40,000 Bride Grooms and 60,000 Brides Could not Singe there Manes."

The reporter read the last few words aloud. "Could not singe their manes."

"He meant they could not sign their names," Superintendent O'Mara explained. "It's a characteristic of Matt's writing that he often mixes up the letters in a word. It's more fascinating to read that way, don't you think?"

"The catacombs, and the brides and bridegrooms," Father Senan remarked, "have, of course, nothing to do with each other. The year 1846, incidentally, was the year of the great famine in Ireland. The fact that Matt recorded the date, July 9, 1584, the day on which the Prince of Orange died, may be significant too. It was in 1884, three hundred years after the assassination of the prince that Matt was, in his own words, cut to the heart, by the friends who wouldn't

158

buy him a drink. It is possible the date he took the pledge was July 9."

The American moved slowly up O'Connell Street after he had left the police chief and the priest. But he did not keep pace with his feet. He was thinking of Matt Talbot in the chill of his room, reading of an old murder and pondering all the tragic consequences of it — the trail of evil it had left in the slime of the centuries.

No murder lays good eggs, but those found in the nests of racial or religious intolerance hatch out eternal flocks of predatory birds.

The coins of new ideas jingled in the reporter's mind. He was as enchanted with them, and with their music, as any traveler striding away from his first foreign-exchange counter with a fistful of strange new silver pieces.

A phrase remembered started the ideas jingling. "Matt was more than just an ex-drinker."

He was, of course, much more than that. Yet it was the drinkers who needed him most. Even more than the millions of men in the labor unions, the tipplers needed him.

"Matt Talbot, pray for drunks."

# 20

THOSE who join Alcoholics Anonymous, the reporter considered, threading his way through home-rushing crowds, do so because they have learned, through tragic sorrows, that they can do nothing of themselves, that they must depend on a Supreme Power — "God as we understand Him" — to stay sober.

The aim of Alcoholics Anonymous is not only physical sobriety, but a high standard of mental and spiritual sobriety as well. A man or woman coming into the organization, which numbers more than 150,000 in the United States, learns many spiritual lessons, including humility and a childlike dependence on that "Power." He learns that in order to maintain his new status as a sober citizen he must take inventory of himself, ask God to remedy his defects and shortcomings, make amends to people he has hurt, seek to know and to do God's will, and carry the gospel of sobriety to other alcoholics.

Some believe the principles of Alcoholics Anonymous contain "all the religion any man needs." Some find the footsteps

f the Saviour there, and the way back to the faiths they
left years, or months, ago. Some find a short cut to the
knowledge and love of God. Some find nothing. To many the
term, "God as we understand Him," is as foggy a mess of
words as "the will of the people . . . the freedom of the
seas . . . the noble experiment . . . the self-determination of
small nations."

There are many Catholics in the United States and Canada
who are steady drinkers, who are alcoholics whether they
realize it or not. Some of them, someday, may come back
to the Church through some such organization as Alcoholics
Anonymous, who are, incidentally, neither alcoholics now, nor
anonymous any more, since God knows them all and loves
them well. Or they may come back through reading about
Matt, or hearing about him, or through somebody's asking
Matt to intercede for them.

They knew the face of God, perhaps, before they took
to drink; and knew it well. But the swizzle stick can distort,
or smear, or obliterate, or caricature a face more effectively
even than a lipstick. (But then, alas! some who frown so
virtuously on the crime of drinking have also forgotten the
look of the Holy Face, if they ever knew it. There are many
things that can rub out or deface or mar an image.)

People rising out of an alcoholic haze, in which there seemed
to be nothing good, grope for the feel of God in relatives and
friends, in doctors and nurses, in uniformed attendants. They
look for Him everywhere, frightened and shamed and confused, not knowing whom they seek. They realize, perhaps they
have made a god of alcohol, and that it is necessary now to
let God replace that idol.

Matt could be a friend and guide to these. Matt could not
only show them God; he could bring God to them, and
them to God.

But the Capuchin was right. Matt was more than just a
patron for ex-drinkers.

He could be an example to many sober people. He could
inspire and guide those who spend all their time and energies

and health at amassing money or intrenching themselves or the heights of power; those who continually eat too much and too expensively and too greedily and too wastefully, and who diet too much, sporadically; those who give their lives to making college graduates and "big shots" out of kids meant to be carpenters or plumbers or mechanics or streetcar conductors; those who let their children grow up with little or no supervision; and those who yawn themselves to death with boredom, or laziness, or sheer plain shiftlessness — or because they are devoid of any kind of vision or imagination.

He could also serve as a brilliant searchlight to illumine the paths of all those engaged in the lay apostolate of Catholic Action, and those of bishops, priests, and nuns!

Matt was a lay apostle, the first great lay apostle of modern times; but it could not be said that he practiced Catholic Action. He worked alone, in secret, hiding his sanctity from all except a few. Catholic Action is group action, trained action, mandated action. It must be organized. It must work with the apostolate of the hierarchy. It must participate in the works of that apostolate.

Matt lived in voluntary poverty; in strict obedience to the laws of God and the Church, in strict obedience, also, to the just orders, rules, and regulations of his employers — and of his union officials — and in a positive masculine chastity. He performed most, if not all, of the corporal and spiritual works of mercy. His goal was the goal of all Catholic Actionists, personal sanctification. His method of achieving that goal was essentially theirs — doing the will of God.

He was a recluse, yet he was more of a "social worker" than many of those engaged exclusively in social work or the so-called "organized charities." He was a bachelor, but many married couples and their families depended on him to solve their problems, domestic, financial, material, spiritual, and romantic. He lived alone, but he loved families, big families. He especially loved children.

He loved priests too. He was, it might be said, a priest himself, mystically. At least he gave Christ, in a sort of mystical

munion, to everyone he met by his charity, by his gentle-
, by his words of warning or advice, by his ready sympathy,
his humility, by his cheerfulness in peace or pain, by his
at love, by the example of his life.

Matt had received all the Sacraments except the "Social
acraments," Marriage and Holy Orders. Yet he could be
f exceptional help, in many ways, to any section of society —
especially to the family and to the priesthood.

It wasn't only through the misuse and abuse of bread and
wine that the devil sought to destroy the United States and
Canada — to make America an easy prey for his Red step-
sons. He was trying to ruin it through the destruction of a
wholesome family life, and by sowing dissension in the ranks
of the priests and nuns.

What was happening to the families of America, those
sturdy, hardy units that had accomplished such great things?
Divorce; birth-prevention techniques, carefully and deliberately fostered; abortions, multiplied every day throughout the
length and breadth of the continent; new ideas of "progress,"
"education," and "self-assertiveness"; and the constantly
increasing menace of juvenile delinquency. That's what was
happening to families.

Family life was disintegrating.

The Holy Father was alarmed. "Restore the family," he
begged the faithful in America. "Above all, work for the
restoration of the family to Christ."

The family and the priesthood! If Lucifer could take those
fortresses, and hold them, what could prevent his adding North
America to his other holdings?

It didn't seem such a hard task. Pit the clergy and the
hierarchy against the laity. Encourage the priests and bishops
to distrust the laity. Urge the laity to distrust and disobey the
bishops and the priests. Divide the clergy themselves, and
conquer. Sow vexation between the old pastors and their
bishops, and between the old pastors and the zealous young
curates. Drive the curates into leaving the Church, if possible,
and into preaching and writing against it and its doctrines.

And the nuns! How Lucifer hates the holy women! Wou
it be easy now — and a sweet revenge — to make them t.
girls were idiotic to go into Catholic Action when they mr
enter the novitiate?

To make the teachers ridicule the lay apostolate and wrec
it before it got really started? — "Sister says only the crack
pots go into Catholic Action."

And then to use St. Paul to the same end. "It is better to
marry than to burn." The nuns might insist to their sweet
girl grads that there were but two real vocations — the convent
or the home. The lay apostolate? Christ in the market place?
The single life dedicated, without vows, to the service of
Christ in the poor?

"Sister says, 'It's better to marry than to burn.' "

Despite the fact that priests were other Christs, and nuns
were the brides of Christ, they were all human. They could
be made to feel they had been indifferently treated by the
laity — though each one of them had come from that same
laity. They could be made to believe they were ill-treated by
their elders, their superiors, their chaplains or pastors, their
bishops, or even the pope himself.

They could be convinced that other religious men and
women were their rivals, their false friends, their dangerous
enemies; that the pope had been fooled into encouraging the
laity to take part in the apostolate of the hierarchy, and that
the bishops were fools for permitting any kind of Catholic
Action in their sees.

But no priest or nun could ever be deceived into thinking
St. Louis Marie had been mistaken when he wrote of the
Blessed Mother — and of the great lay saints that were to
come "in the latter days."

"God the Holy Ghost wishes to form Himself in her (Mary)
and to form elect for Himself by her," St. Louis wrote, "and
He has said to her . . . 'reproduce yourself in My elect, that
I may behold in them with complacence the roots of your
invincible faith, of your profound humility, of your universal
mortification, and all your virtues. You are always My spouse,

aithful, as pure, and as fruitful as ever. Let your faith
Me My faithful, your purity My virgins, and your
.ility My Temples and My elect.' "

No priest or nun would say Matt Talbot, St. Louis' disciple,
was not a temple of the Holy Ghost, was not one of the elect
ormed in Mary by the Holy Ghost. And every priest and every
nun could see that the laity, having produced such an excep-
tionally holy servant of God, might yield hundreds of thousands of others; just as anyone would know that, if you found
a nugget in a gully anywhere you might find a million others;
and, if you took the trouble to dig, you might uncover a vein
of solid gold. Chalices can be made of that gold, to be filled,
and to be offered to the Lord.

Matt must know that the devil was attacking these two
fortresses, these two holy "Social Sacraments," not only to
wreck America and leave it flat and burning, but also to mock
almighty God, as he mocked Him through bread and wine.

"Let your priests and nuns and lay Catholics work together
for God, in peace and unity," the reporter could almost hear
Matt saying. "I learned, the hard way, what strength there
is in unity. Workers of the world, unite. Catholics of the world,
unite. Catholics of America, unite and chase the devil out of
the United States and Canada."

He could hear him adding a few words to that. "And mind
what my friend, Father Patrick Peyton says to you: the family
that prays together stays together; pray the Rosary."

It was wonderful to listen to the music of those coins picked
up in Dublin after a chat with a layman and a priest.

What would they buy at home?

# 21

AT THE Catholic mission in Granby Lane one can obtain statues of saints and angels, books, holy pictures, Rosaries, crucifixes, and other religious articles. One can also buy Irish Sweepstakes tickets, and meet people who knew Matt Talbot, or knew about him.

The mission is operated by Susan Purcell and her niece Miss Molly Morphy. It is run not so much for profits, if any, as for the accommodation of worshipers going to St. Saviour Church and people wishing to know about Matt Talbot.

It is a sort of rallying place for Matt's closest and most devoted friends, for pilgrims from various parts of the world, and especially for those who wish to spread devotion to the "holy man in overalls."

"I felt I owed it to Matt," Miss Purcell explained to the visitor, "to open this sort of place, and right on this spot. I met the man once. It was a raw and gusty day. He was coming from the church, and I was going toward it. We met here in Granby Lane. As I approached him the wind blew his overskirts this way and that and I saw his bare knees sticking from his trousers.

I wasn't scandalized. But I was indignant. Such a vulgar d needless display. If the man had no woman to sew up .e rents in those trousers, and no decent trousers to put on, 1en, I said to myself, let him take needle and thread and mend them himself. What did he think he was? A ballerina? A Scotsman? If he were a Scot, then let him wear a kilt over his bare knees. It was an outrage for a man to go around the streets like that, half naked as it were.

"God have mercy on my soul! How do you think I felt when it came to me that the little man I scolded so furiously in my mind was none other than the saintly Matthew Talbot? How do you think I felt when it dawned on me that he had deliberately cut the cloth of his knees so that he would not have it so soft, kneeling for hours at a time before the altar of the Lord, or on the rough wood planks of his hard bed?"

She produced a sort of ledger and opened it for the visitor's benefit.

"Rash judgment is a terrible sin," she said. "I decided to devote my life to promoting Matt Talbot's cause. Would you like to write your name and address here? You'll find thousands of names there already. People from most any place in the world. There was a girl in here not long ago, the one who wrote a book about that darling St. Maria Goretti. She came right from Italy."

"Marie Cecilia Buehrle?" the newspaperman asked.

"The very one," Miss Purcell exclaimed, delighted that the author's name was known. "She had talked to Mamma Assunta, the saint's mother, and Mamma Goretti said she hoped Matt Talbot too would be raised to the altar soon. Wasn't that nice? But then people even in the wilds of Africa know about Matt and pray for his canonization, and people in the Pacific islands, and people in Russia and China and Japan and many other countries you wouldn't think ever heard of Matt."

"The idea that an ordinary man, a union man, a striker in

his time, could be regarded as a saint by anybody, asto
the whole world," the visitor said, glancing at names
the book.

"We have heaps and heaps of newspaper cuttings som
where," Miss Purcell went on, "about Matt Talbot. Favor
attributed to him, and the strange ways some people took t
honor him. There is one story I must tell you about. And
don't laugh. Father Dolan laughed when I talked about that
woman. You know Father Dolan?"

"The Carmelite priest who wrote about Matt?"

"That's the one. I told him about the woman who visits
Matt's grave every morning as soon as the gates open, says
her prayers, and goes away. She is as faithful in attendance as
Matt was at early Mass. Nobody ever found out who she is
or where she lives. Nobody ever got a word out of her. I
told Father Dolan I thought it was the girl who wanted to
marry Matt, the minister's cook, poor darling. He roared.
But it might be, just the same."

The visitor bought a Sweepstakes ticket.

"We've been pretty lucky," Miss Morphy said. "We've got
several winners in the past few years. If our tickets are among
the winners we get bonuses. We got 500 pounds sterling the
year Caughoo won the Derby. We've had some other staggering
checks. Miss Purcell wrote her name on the back of each one
and handed it over to a charity, asking the nun or the priest —
whichever was in charge — to pray for Matt Talbot's canonization. Have you been to the grave in Glasnevin?"

"Not yet," the reporter said. "Is it far?"

"I'll take you there Sunday," Miss Morphy said. "You
might get lost. You'd get lost surely in the cemetery itself,
unless you followed the crowds. We go out there every Sunday
morning to decorate the grave."

Several women came in, as Miss Morphy concluded the
business of the Sweepstakes. They bore armfuls of fresh-cut
flowers they had grown for the sole purpose of decorating
Matt's grave.

"They'll be fresh," Miss Purcell promised.

ss Purcell, and some friends, it developed, kept the
s on the Granby Lane shrine filled with fresh flowers.
. Anna Keogh and her son Joseph, who had gone to
tt's assistance when he fell dying that June morning
enty-seven years before, had set up the shrine. Miss Purcell,
iss Morphy, and others devoted to Matt keep it always
eady for the pilgrims.

It was in the Catholic mission the newspaperman met
Martha Doyle, one night. Miss Doyle is Matt's cousin. Her
mother was a sister of Charles Talbot, Matt's father.

It was Miss Doyle who let him copy from the prayer book
that came to her from Matt's sister Susan, Matt's favorite
prayer after Mass . . . "O good Jesus, accept this Holy Communion as my viaticum . . . "

"Would you like to copy down another prayer Matt loved?"
she asked. "It's called, 'Invocation of the seven glorious angels
who stand before the throne of God.' Or this one, called 'A
prayer in time of trial'? Or these under the heading of 'Devotion to the Holy Ghost'? Matt burned with the love of the
Holy Ghost. But then, if you love Mary, how can you help
loving the Holy Ghost?"

"Did you know your cousin well?" the reporter asked.

Miss Doyle looked sad, and shook her head.

"I was just a child," she said. "I know he liked me. My
mother told me so. I was his favorite, she said. But then,
sure, he loved everybody. Maybe we were all his favorites.
No, I don't remember him very well, nor know much about
him. Still, one story does stay in my mind. It's the one about
the wild party in the tenement house, with everybody dancing
reels and jigs and sets and squares and all. Matt was about
sixteen or seventeen at the time, and not interested at all in
the dancing.

"What interested Matt was the liquor situation. He didn't
think the available stores would go very far. He felt he should
do something about it. So he turned to a friend and said,
'I don't know how, but I'm going to get out of here.' It did
seem impossible, with everybody between him and the door,

and them dancing and stamping and having the tim.
their lives.

"You know how he managed? He got down on his kr.
and snaked his way through the dancers, pinching any an.
that got in his way. And his friend with him! Out they wer
and spent all the silver they had on a stock of liquor the;
thought would last the night.

"The story is true, and typical of the man. He always
wanted people around him to have enough. Enough of everything. He always wanted them to be happy. He was a merry
sort of fellow. He laughed a lot, even when he was sick. He
was merry in God. You know what he'd say, looking at the
windows of this mission?

"He'd look at a statue, and he'd say, 'Is that chalk?' and
then he'd say, like as not, 'The saints are all dead in there,
but they're all alive in heaven.' He was forever talking about
the saints, saying things like that. I've heard so many things
about him! How he fed the birds. What a funny little
mustache he had. How he always used an old-fashioned straight
razor. The way people sneaked up to his door sometimes and
peeked through the keyhole at him. How some woman, not
Miss Purcell, asked Matt one day if she couldn't take his
trousers — and him home in bed — and put a stitch in them
where his knees showed. I've heard many things since he
died. How many people wanted a sliver from the planks of
his bed to cure themselves of every disease under the sun.
How Susan once put Matt's coat on a man — was it Mc-
Guinness that was? and changed his life? And I heard, or
read somewhere, that the Sunday before he died, Matt was
walking with Willie Larkin, the president of his sodality, and
he said there should be a statue, or a picture, of the Sacred
Heart set up in the heart of Dublin — a sort of municipal
enthronement, if you please. He spoke of all the good that
would come of it.

" 'God blesses those who honor His Sacred Heart,' he told
Willie Larkin, 'wouldn't He bless Dublin now, if we honored
Him with a shrine in the middle of O'Connell Street? Wouldn't

likely, make the whole of Ireland a grand free nation, for
wonderful thing done for Him in its capital? Willie, Dublin
uld become the finest city in the world, and every working-
an would benefit.'

"He always thought every workingman should have his
own home and his own garden. But when it came to himself,
it was different. He got rid of his money as soon as he could,
spending as little as possible on himself. He almost never
bought anything to wear. God would outfit him with the
clothes he should wear, he said. Why should he worry about
such things? God would give him all he needed."

"God," said Miss Purcell, "gives everything to everybody,
and He knows who to give what to, and when. He's been a
long time at it, and He's efficient."

It was in the Catholic mission, a few nights later, that the
reporter listened to the beautiful stories told by Mrs. Sweeney.

# 22

SOME years after Matt's death, Willie Larkin managed, despite considerable opposition, to have a shrine opened in Dublin to pay honor to the Sacred Heart.

Once it was up, it seems, there was no more opposition. There were even processions winding through the streets, and thousands of men and women marching with Rosaries in their hands, or lighted candles, or pictures of the Sacred Heart, or the Immaculate Heart, or of their favorite saints.

The shrine contains a picture of the Sacred Heart, and also a picture of Our Lady of Fatima. It is in the middle of O'Connell Street, directly opposite the Gresham Hotel, one of the most prominent hostelries in the city. There is a cab stand there, and a row of taxis always waiting.

A taxi driver wiped the dust off the glass that covered the yearning face of Christ, but desisted when he saw the newspaperman approaching. He pretended he had noticed the picture for the first time, and that it didn't mean anything particular to him.

172

"That?" he said. "That picture? Oh, that's been there a ng time, sir. Before I started hacking. All I know is, it's here. You want a cab, sir?"

The drivers keep fresh flowers in front of the picture, and see that vigil lights burn there at night. Not one of them, officially, knows anything about the shrine. But it would be well for a man to show a great respect for it. Or else!

The newspaperman didn't want a cab. He wanted merely to see the shrine Matt Talbot's loving mind had given his native land, his native people. He looked at it a long time, then decided to walk down O'Connell Street, and back.

This was a clean and prosperous-looking city. He noticed that for the first time. It had once been known as "dear old dirty Dublin." But the Irish didn't own it then.

It was one of the cleanest cities in the world, one of the busiest, one of the most thriving. God most certainly had blessed it!

The visitor walked for blocks. He saw no drunks, no beggars, no man who looked like he might be a thief, no woman who didn't seem to be an honest, decent woman.

He recalled an interview he had had with Benito Mussolini, an odd little man in a cheap blue suit who, at the time, had more power than any king in Europe, Africa, or Asia.

"Have you seen any drunkards in Italy?" Mussolini had asked, rubbing his bristly blue jowls to call attention to his pile-driver chin. "Have you seen any beggars, any bad women, any murderers or thieves?"

He made gestures as he talked, to indicate that he threw drunks and prostitutes into dungeons, manacled beggars, and lined thieves and murderers against a wall and shot them.

He was being ironic because, at that time, in the United States, the mightiest and the richest and the "driest" nation in history, there were so many drunks, streetwalkers, beggars, thieves, and murderers the citizens couldn't build jails enough to hold them all.

Poor little Mussolini who used to fill his followers with false hope and pride, and his enemies with castor oil, who used to

**173**

march little boys in regiments down the spotless streets of Rome to make real killers of them!

Poor little ambitious dictator, hanging naked and head down like a butchered hog, to delight a crowd of drunken men and women who had once regarded him as a god!

The newspaperman came slowly back toward his hotel. No. There were no drunks, no strange women, no beggars. There were no dictators either. Nor police spies. No regiments of goose-stepping little black-shirted boys.

Ireland was, for the most part, as free as the United States!

Who, besides God, was responsible for all this? Daniel O'Connell? Robert Emmett? Charles Parnell? Patrick Pearse? Big Jim Larkin? Eamon de Valera? All of them, and others? And Matt Talbot?

Matt had never made a speech, jockeyed a law through a hostile parliament, handled a rifle, or thrown a bomb. But maybe he was right when he said that the most effective weapon is love — prayer, self-sacrifice, self-immolation.

There was a sign in a grocer's window. "Food parcels for England." And there were many people inside buying meats and vegetables and candies and nuts and raisins and flour and sugar and eggs and cereals for friends and relatives in rationed Britain.

Who had brought this abundance to Ireland, the nation that still talked of its years of famine? Who, besides God? Was it some wild boyo with a bayonet forninst the Adam's apple of the foe? Was it some clever politician with the gift of gab? Was it some economic genius as yet unknown to fame? Or was it an ex-drunkard on his knees?

The American, unmindful of the crowds, bumped into a fellow stroller, who begged his pardon. The Irish voice is soft and gentle, with a music all its own. It makes the English language melodious. And in Dublin it has no brogue. If one does hear an Irish accent in the city, it is a Kerry man speaking, or a lass from Cork, or maybe an old lady from the rocks of Donegal.

"Ah," said the Irishman, " 'tis easy to see the thoughts of

174

American, and him looking at Lord Nelson high over all us — God be good to the poor ignorant sailor soul he was — and wondering why we don't put Father Matthew in his place."

"Matthew Talbot," the visitor corrected him. "Not Father Matthew. The little Capuchin has a statue of his own up the street. Why not put Matt Talbot up there on Nelson's pillar?"

"Matt Talbot?" The Irishman was puzzled. "And American, was he?"

"He was born and brought up in Dublin," the reporter said, "and he's buried in Glasnevin. He was a worker in a lumber-yard when he died, a little old bare-noggined guy nobody ever noticed until after he was buried — to give you an American idea of an Irish bull. People come from the ends of the earth to see his grave. And there are people right here who never heard of him?"

"Ah," the Irishman said, walking away, "and isn't it like us, not to treasure our own?"

Across the street, stacked on a sort of handcart or "book barrow," were piles of Catholic newspapers, magazines, and books. Young men and women, evidently members of the Legion of Mary, stood by, ready to sell, or give, these wares to all who asked for them.

The visitor wondered if Matt had had anything to do with the founding of the Legion of Mary. The Legion had been started in 1921. It had flowered out of the slavery of Jesus in Mary, as taught by St. Louis Marie, and as taught by Matt Talbot also.

The Legion of Mary! The American stood still. He was watching fierce Red armies marching through the streets of Chinese cities. He was listening to the stories of fugitive bishops, priests, nuns, and ordinary lay people. He was thrilling to tales of "Sing-Mo-Malya," the Virgin Queen more feared by Asia's Communists than any atom bomb.

Who was this woman, the Red lords asked, who had turned so many Chinese hearts against the government of the kindly Mao Tse-tung? Who was this woman terrible as an army arrayed in battle, this formidable maiden-mother who thought she could make herself the mother and queen of Chi

And who were these imperialist foreign-devil spies who h
so affected Chinese youths that they willingly and gladly e
dured excruciating tortures, and even lingering deaths, for th
love of that fair woman? They were growing in numbers, and ir
daring, every day. Good Communists might exile, jail, or kill
thousands of them, and they could banish or murder all the missionaries, but they could not kill the Legion. There was heart-
filling, heart-swelling, heart-lifting rapture in that thought.

And, for all anybody knew to the contrary, the reporter
mused, much the same sort of missionary work was being
carried on by Legionnaires in Russia and Poland and Yugo-
slavia and other moral deserts.

How vital it was for the layman to make himself as holy
and as zealous as any priest or nun, and to work as hard to
spread the faith! How tremendously important, in this bar-
baric age, the lay apostolate had become! What a stupendous
duty had been given each Catholic man and woman — the duty
of becoming a great saint.

The missionaries were gone from Asia, or only their bones
remained in its soil. Lay people, ordinary lay people, were
carrying on their work. They were grouped together, where
they could work without too much interference. In other places
they were working alone, as Matt had worked, fasting, praying, doing penances of many kinds, spreading the sweet names
of Jesus and Mary, giving Christ to all.

How big a man was this slave of Mary who once had been
the slave of alcohol? How great was he in the eyes of God?
How great would he become in the eyes of men? How big
could a man get, praying and doing penance day and night for
more than forty years?

There were hundreds of thousands of lay apostles today, the
stroller reflected, performing an infinite variety of "Catholic
Action" duties. Matt was the first of them to die in "these
latter days."

Is it possible that Catholic Action, as we know it in all its
many manifestations in this generation, came out of Matt Tal-

s grave? Could the life of one poor workingman produce
.h spiritual riches? What limits of sanctity can an ordinary
an attain? Or are there any limits?

"You are the Church," Pius XI had said, "you Catholic lay
people. You must not consider the Church as the pope, the
bishops, and the priests, with yourselves as a sort of outer
fringe. . . . You are the Church . . . just as my hands are my
body. . . . It is only through you that the Church can adapt
herself to the changing conditions in the world. . . . Go forth
to conquer the world again for Christ!"

The people had gone forth, especially the people of the
Legion. They had gone forth to conquer and to die. Many of
them had died, as gloriously as the martyrs under Nero and
other tyrants. Were these the saints St. Louis Marie had
predicted?

It seemed fitting that the Legion had been born in Ireland,
a nation dear to Mary, and a country that had sent its missionaries all over the world in the early centuries of the faith,
to civilize and Christianize it. It was good to know the missionaries of this day were lay people.

The stroller went across the street to the young people standing near the book barrow. He must find out what — if anything — Matt had to do with the Legion.

"Have you any books on Matt Talbot and the Legion?" he
inquired.

A pretty girl looked up at him, puzzled.

"Matt Talbot? Who is he? Should I know him?"

"Indeed you should," the reporter said.

The girl thought hard. "Oh I think I know," she said.
"Isn't he the patron saint of Dublin?"

The visitor bought two little books and went his way without answering the pretty Legionary's question. One was called
*Terrible as an Army*. The other was *John A. McGuinness*. He
thrust them into the side pocket of his coat, intending to read
them at his leisure. Maybe they had something to do with
Matt, maybe not. He'd find out, later, why he had chosen just
those two from all the others.

# 23

IN THE Granby Lane mission, one June night, the reporter was permitted to come close to the personality, the power, the sweetness, the austerity, and the grandeur of Matt Talbot. This was while Mrs. Ann Sweeney sat on a stool and talked to him, and to Miss Purcell and Miss Morphy.

Mrs. Sweeney, the mother of sixteen children, met Matt Talbot when she was a small girl. She never spoke to him. But few people have ever known him so well as she does. The spirit of the man emanates from her as naturally as perfume from a rose, as she talks. She talks for hours; and the listener is amazed, when she gets up to go; for it seems as if she had only begun to talk.

She talks of Matt constantly. She talks to him constantly. She writes about him, in poetry and prose. She dreams of him. She longs for him, as a holy nun longs for St. Joseph, say, St. Aloysius, or the Archangel Michael. And she attends to his affairs — besides taking care of her husband, her household, and the fourteen children still living.

178

...rs. Sweeney is in her early or middle forties, though she ...s younger. She speaks softly, calmly, without any effort, ...hout attempting any drama. But now and then the wistful ...te comes into her voice. As for instance when she says ...mething like:

"Seventeen years I've been away from that room. Seventeen long years. It broke my heart to leave it. Ah, it did break the heart of me. But I had to go. I had to. And I'll never go back to it! I couldn't go back to it now!"

She lived in Matt's neighborhood when she was a child. She used to see Matt passing her house. He always avoided the main thoroughfares, she said, "lest his sense of hearing or seeing should be turned away from the voice and the face of God.

"He always went the byways and backways because they were the quiet ways," she said, "and the sure ways of avoiding shameful sights and ungodly noises. On his way to work he visited the Church of St. Joseph, in Portland Row, and was observed to light seven candles daily at the shrine of Our Lady of Lourdes. That is something I've never told anybody else.

"He walked with his eyes lowered. He never noticed me. He seemed to see only the children on the street, especially those who ran toward him. But there was an old blind lady he'd always stop and talk to. She used to sit out on her front stoop every morning, smoking her pipe, and wait for him. He usually had a pinch of tobacco for her.

"He was always poorly dressed, but there was such a dignity about him nobody minded his clothes. I was always impressed with him.

"I lived nearer to his room in Upper Rutland Street after I married. My husband used to see him nearly every summer morning. My husband and poor old Sally McDonald, the fish woman.

"My husband nearly knocked Matt down with his bicycle, one morning at 5:30. 'Cross of God,' he said, 'did I hurt you, Mr. Talbot?' Matt merely remarked, 'It's a glorious morning, Postman,' and went on. And Sally blessed herself.

"Sally used to come out at the same time, for the mark
wheeling a three-wheeled barrow. She'd greet Matt cordial
and then she'd turn to my husband and say, 'That's a gran
man. Off to Mass, and it like cockcrow! And then to earn h.
bread with the sweat of his brow while the rest of us are
sleeping our senses away.'

"Many the time I heard Sally's voice saying a word or two
like that, and then I'd hear the rumble of her barrow going
down Rutland Street, over the cobble stones. She too was
going to earn her bread with the sweat of her brow, and it
like cockcrow. Matt never answered her greetings, except with
a pleasant nod of the head.

"We moved into Matt's room, my husband and I and the
babies, a few weeks after Matt died. There were dozens of
people wanting the place. We were the lucky ones. No one
will ever know what that room meant to me. It was a little
palace, for all it was so small and cold and dark.

"When the family kept getting bigger and bigger we had to
get more rooms. We managed to get some adjoining Matt's,
and I tried to keep the children out of that place. But it was
impossible, of course, and then I couldn't help but think it
did them good just to be there.

"The strange thing is that there was always a great peace
in that room, and a great comfort, even when it was full of
visitors. You'd think a woman with a growing family wouldn't
have time to show visitors the room where Matt had lived
so long, and to tell them all about him. But, somehow I
always managed.

"I was enchanted with the room from the first moment I
stepped into it. There were two old Rosaries there, and a
number of medals, and a few holy pictures. I loved them. I was
even excited to touch the bread crumbs Matt had left in the
cupboard, and the pinches of cocoa and sugar, and the old
blue enamel teapot.

"So many things happened in that room! I had seven children
there. I met the shadow of death three times. I entertained
hosts of priests there, and a bishop, and a cardinal.

180

# MATT TALBOT

'It was in 1932, when the Eucharistic Congress was held in ᴜblin, that the cardinal came. Cardinal Verdier, Archbishop ᴏf Paris. I didn't expect him at all. I was frying my husband's ᴅinner when a priest came to tell me that I would be visited that night by a prince of the Church!

"I forgot about the dinner. I forgot about the baby, then six months old or so. I forgot about my husband, and everything else. Down on my knees I went and started to scrub the floor.

"My husband came home late and found me with the scrub pail, and no dinner waiting. He was mad. 'Cross of God!' he said. 'Is it crazy you are, Annie Sweeney? Cleaning the floor and no dinner ready.' "Hold your whisht,' I told him, 'and go out and buy a few flowers.' Oh, he was sure then that I was out of my mind. Flowers, was it? And him that hungry he could hardly stand up. So I had to tell him then about the prince of the Church.

"It was supposed to be a secret, but himself had scarce got to the bottom of the stairs than Mary Murphy, a child of fifteen or sixteen, walked in and asked 'Is it true?' 'Who told you?' I asked her. 'I overheard you talking to himself,' she said; and with that out she ran to tell the neighbors.

"I was in tears when my husband came back with the flowers. 'Go and get a carpet for the floor,' I said. 'Cross of God,' said he, but he went and got the loan of a carpet. 'If you spot it,' the woman said who loaned it, 'I'll sue you.' What a night! Himself without supper. The children without supper. And the crowd growing and growing outside 'til I didn't dare send my husband or the children out of the flat again for anything.

"The police came, and they held back the crowd. They wouldn't let my own mother past them. Nor Matt's two sisters. Ah sure the crowd was out for my poor man's blood; and mine too.

"And then, suddenly, the great man came, and he gave his blessing to all the people down below, and he came upstairs in his beautiful scarlet robes, and knelt down and prayed for

181

ten or fifteen minutes; not on the carpet, either, but on t.
bare hard floor. Thank God I'd had the sense to scrub
clean for him.

"It was a long time before people forgave me for shutting
them out that night. What heart scalds one endures!

"Another night, about 11 o'clock, we were saying the Rosary
in Matt's room when a neighbor knocked at the door. 'There's
a lovely gentleman below,' she said, 'all in scarlet and gold,
would be saying a few prayers with you, if you please.'

"It was a bishop from Australia. He finished three decades
with us, kneeling upright on the floor. And he said, before
he gave us his blessing and went away — he said, 'You don't
know what is in the corners of this room!' With that he put
his hand on the bed, as though to touch a holy relic."

Customers came into the mission as Mrs. Sweeney talked.
Miss Purcell or Miss Morphy waited on them. At midnight
Miss Morphy locked the door on the inside, and turned the
window lights low. The newspaperman asked a question or
two, and Mrs. Sweeney began to talk about the Legion of Mary.

"The idea for the formation of the Legion," she said, "came
from the brilliant mind of a Dutch Jesuit who was, for ten
years, a constant visitor to Matt's room. He heard of the
simple little ceremony Matt used in enrolling people in the
chains. Matt spread St. Louis Marie's book about True Devotion everywhere in Dublin, and he enrolled at least thirty in
the chains of slavery. I got the story when I visited an old
crippled lady, Mary Hopkins, who wore chains around her
neck. The Dutch Jesuit, Father T. Pepperkorn, knew Mary too.

"Mary Hopkins lived in a stable in Sarsfield Street. She
got the chains from Matt in 1912, or 1913, or thereabouts — a
long time before she died. She died of cancer. I nursed her. I
visited her quite often. She knew even the day she was going
to die. She died on a feast day of our Lady. Before she died
she said I was to have the plaque of St. Theresa — the one
with the Child Jesus giving the saint some beautiful roses. I
didn't want to take it. 'Do what I tell you,' she said. So I
got a pair of pliers and took it from its bracket. Then she said

. was to have two of the links from her neck chain, and I was to wear them on my own neck.

"Father Pepperkorn obtained a lot of information about Matt from Mary Hopkins. And he, together with a Mr. Sullivan, I believe, and a Mr. Metcalf, and Frank Duff, and then Miss Martin — I should say, rather, Rev. Mother Mary Martin — formed the Legion. Rev. Mother Martin is the daughter of Thomas Martin, one of Matt's employers; and she is also the foundress of the Medical Sisters of Mary, saintly doctors and nurses who do missionary work all over the world today.

"Despite what may be said to the contrary, these are the facts, and Matt is the founder of the Legion."*

Mrs. Sweeney talked of the relics she sends to people all over the world. She "inherited" a lot of wood — the bed planks, the log pillow, the floor boards, the cupboards and their shelves. She cuts them up — what's left of them — encases them in cellophane and leather, with a picture of Matt, and mails them out. She believes that miracles may result from the use of any one of those tiny bits of board. And only miracles will lead to Matt's canonization.

She gave up some of these treasures to the Archbishop of Dublin. An American priest cadged most of what was left.

"He said to me, 'For the love of the Mother of God, give

---

*Months after he had talked to Mrs. Sweeney, the newspaperman received a letter from Frank Duff, the head of the Legion, in which he said Matt had "actually . . . no association of any kind with the Legion."

"Among those who began the Legion," Mr. Duff wrote, "there was not even one person who knew Matt Talbot. . . . I did know of him. One of my very particular friends at that time was a Mr. Raphael O'Callaghan, who was the only person who knew Matt Talbot, that is to say outside his own family circle and his fellow-workmen. Raphael O'Callaghan was prodigiously interested in Matt, visited him frequently, lent him books and explained them to him, and otherwise discussed religious topics with him.

"Undoubtedly Raphael O'Callaghan played a vital part in the development of Matt Talbot. This forms an interesting exemplification of the role which all of us can play in apostleship. It is possible for us to go to people who are far superior to ourselves in virtue, and yet to accomplish great things for those people. . . . It was through O'Callaghan that the world knows of Matt Talbot at all."

me the planks and the shelves.' What could I say, and Mat sitting there beside me, so close I could feel his breath, and he in heaven? The priest took the boards away with him. And my life with them!

"We had no locks on the place and I was always afraid that some other souvenir hunters would come in and help themselves. I had reason to be afraid, too. Once three brothers came into the room, three hoodlums bent on sacrilege and theft. It just happened my husband was there at the time, and the room was dark.

"The thieves didn't see him. They were quite bold. 'You see that wall?' one said. 'Twelve times a night a black cross comes out of that wall. We'll cut a square out of it, and sell it for relics.' It was then my husband spoke up.

" 'Cross of God!' he said, 'what are you doing here?'

"The three of them screamed like one. 'O my God!' they screamed; and they went tearing out of the room and down the stairs, dropping their knives — and one of them dropped a prayer book as well. They swore it was Matt had chased them.

"Sometime after the cardinal had gone the neighbors began to complain about all the poor drunks that were coming to Matt's room. They said I should close the door and keep it closed. They said I was hurting Matt's cause.

"I knew it was gossip, and I knew it was bad feeling. There was talk that the cardinal and the bishop had given me enough money to stuff Nelson's pillar, that I had gold stacked up to the ceiling somewhere. One night I sent a relative out with an old tick the children couldn't use any more. And didn't the story come back to me that it was a tea chest of gold I got from the cardinal? I was sick of it all. I went to Father Murphy and I went to Father McGarigle. And I told them about the neighbors. They threw up their arms in horror. 'Who in the name of God said that?' they wanted to know. And they said, 'Sit down, woman, and dry your eyes, and let you be easy in your foolish heart. Nuns and priests? Keep them out. But poor old sinners? Poor old drunkards? Leave the door open for them. And don't mind anything that's said.'

184

I had to leave the room at last. I was going to have my tenth ...d. We had to get out of Rutland Street. We had to have ...re space. And I fought with myself about it. And I fought ...th Matt. And he with me. 'You're not to go away from me,' Matt kept saying. But I was going away.

"One day I lay down in Matt's bed, and told my husband to get the children out of the way and go for the doctor. This time I never felt a single pain. And the baby was perfect. I called her Theresa, after Matt's favorite. And, when I could, I went to Father McGarigle and told him I had to go and leave Matt, though Matt wanted me to stay.

" 'Forget the room,' Father McGarigle said. 'Forget the room, woman dear, and go straight away out of it. You're not leaving Matt. He'll stay in your memory and your heart forever. You're only leaving the room.'

" 'But he keeps tormenting me to stay,' I said.

"Father McGarigle showed me the confessional in the church. 'Matt knelt there,' he said. 'He knelt there every Saturday. You'll not forget him. Nor will I. Go on doing the good work. Wherever you go, Matt will go with you.'

"One day, months after I'd left the room I ran into an old friend. I hadn't seen her in years. 'Folks tell me you left Matt Talbot's place,' she said. 'Are you gone mad, Annie?' 'Yes,' I said, 'I've left. I must have been mad. I'm on my way to confession. Will you come with me?'

"She startled me. 'I wouldn't dare,' she said. 'The priest would never give me absolution. He never would. It's going to hell I am, Annie Sweeney, and all your prayers, not mine, won't stop me.

" 'God be good,' I said. 'What is it, Nan?' 'It's the thirty shillings,' she said. 'The thirty pieces of silver. I went to see Matt Talbot once. I was desperate. The rent was due and I had a bailiff's notice. I was sure my five little children and myself would be on the street the next day or the day after. I went to Matt, I don't know why. To this day I don't know why. I was frightened. I knocked twice on his door before he answered. And the way he looked at me — it took me aback. I was

terrified of him. I told him about the bailiff's notice, and ab
my children, and he put the silver into my hand.'

" 'And you never paid it back,' I said.

" 'Not a penny of it. It's many a hungry day I had. Befor
I could think of paying it back I heard he had dropped dead
And him a saint! And me — even in the next world I'll never
be able to pay him back. We'll not be neighbors, Annie. I'll
fry in hell for those thirty poor little pieces of silver!'

" 'Nonsense,' I said, 'Matt would be the last man in heaven
or earth to press you for that money. Give it to the poor, when
you can. Come on to confession with me now, and the priest
will give you absolution. I'll guarantee it.'

" 'You took a load off my mind,' Nan said, 'now tell me how
you came to leave Matt's room.'

"I couldn't tell her. I wept.

"I wept for seven years."

# 24

FOR days the man from America wandered about the streets of Dublin, wandered and wondered. Many generations of his family had prayed to see this day and had not seen it. Ireland in the full glory of her nationhood. Would he ever see it in the glory of her full nationhood? He visited Matt's old room. He visited the Martins' lumberyards, and heard the rattle of the winches, and the mewing of the sea gulls over the green Liffey, and the curses of foreign seamen. He talked to some of Matt's old friends, and got nothing from them. He learned that there was a Matt Talbot Circle, a Matt Talbot League, a Matt Talbot Club, a Matt Talbot Missionary Workers organization, and other similar organizations, all dedicated to the work of spreading devotion to their patron, speeding his canonization, and sanctifying their members. He learned that a temperance movement, the Pioneer Total Abstinence Association of the Sacred Heart was growing like a jungle vine all through Ireland.

"I am sure the example of Matt Talbot is responsible for the

187

fact that so many Irishmen have quit drinking," said a young man wearing the Pioneer pin in the lapel of his coat, "and for the fact that so many others, like myself, have pledged ourselves to total abstinence. We are not for anything like Prohibition such as you had in America — by the way, did you know any of the Prohibition gangsters? — but we are for temperance."

An editorial in the Pioneer magazine for June, 1952, makes this clear. "Pioneers resent being constantly depicted as Prohibitionists and 'kill-joys.' . . . Our sacrifice is inspired by loyalty to Jesus Christ. We have given ourselves to His service, to spread His cause, and to defend His interests. We work to protect innocent children, to safeguard the sanctity of the home, to preserve human dignity, and to protect the morality of our people. . . . Instead of adopting a negative anti-drink policy, ours is a positive approach. 'For Thy greater glory and consolation — for Thy sake to give good example — to practice self-denial — to make reparation to Thee — for the conversion of excessive drinkers.' "

Matt, it seemed, was still working quietly in his apostolate.

The visitor had no trouble finding public houses — though there weren't nearly as many of them as there were bookstores and religious-goods shops. They were quite different from the rum parlors at home. So were the people in them.

They were quiet, friendly, even gracious rooms. The drinkers were mostly workingmen. They seemed to enjoy themselves. They were leisurely about their drinking. There were no women present. No shrill babble was heard. There was no crowd of commuters lined up against the bar demanding a "quick one" before the 5:16 or the 6:03. These people weren't drinking just to get drunk, just to "get an edge on," just to be sociable, or just to show a customer a good time and make a sale. There was nothing American in their drinking.

On the Saturday night before he took the plane home, the visitor was distracted by a street preacher, close to the Nelson pillar. The man was quoting words from the Old Testament to a small half circle of unenthusiastic idlers. He belonged,

188

evidently, to one of those weird sects one never clearly identifies.

For years this particular American, prowling the streets of cities old and new, at late hours of the night, had listened to many street preachers, always in the hope of hearing one quoting from the New Testament, even when it was altered from Matthew, Mark, Luke, and John, into Luther, Knox, Calvin, or Wesley. For years he had loaned his ears patiently, expecting to hear, "And the Lord said unto Luther — or Calvin — or somebody else — 'Thou art a rock, and on this rock I will build my church.'" He had never heard it. He had never heard anything like it. He had never heard anything except abstruse and unintelligent and uninteresting "readings" from the Old Testament.

There could be no profit from this poor tame preacher. How pitiful he looked, standing there, trying to convert the Irish away from Christ and Mary to himself. If all the power of Elizabeth, and Cromwell, and other noted reformers, had failed to shake the Catholics in Ireland in eight hundred and some odd years, what could this strange mouthy man accomplish?

He accomplished one thing. He said something that reminded the visitor of the unread pamphlets in his coat pocket.

At his hotel, sitting near a window that looked down upon the shrine of the Sacred Heart, the reporter learned, from the pamphlet entitled *Terrible as an Army,* that the beginning of the Legion of Mary was "almost accidental."

"Myra House, Francis street, Dublin, was the scene of the birth of Mary's Legion. Shortly after that house had been secured by the Society of St. Vincent de Paul, a branch of the Pioneer Temperance Association was formed to work in the south of the city. . . . It was realized . . . that their meetings should have a definite form, definite prayers, and a system of reports in order to maintain a keen interest in the work. These things were introduced. The opening prayers were taken from the St. Vincent de Paul prayer-card with the addition of five decades of the Rosary; then there was a spiritual reading. . . .

"One of the frequent topics of discussion was St. Louis Marie de Montfort's 'True Devotion to Mary.' The idea was very unusual then — almost unknown in fact — and not clearly grasped even by those of the group who were prominent in proposing the devotion . . . we were ardent in sympathy with it. . . . Then at once the Legion happened. . . .

"There were fifteen ladies and a Vincent de Paul brother present with Father Toher. What was their surprise to see that She whose name they were to bear was there before them! When they came into the room the table 'round which they were to meet, and which was usually bare, was decked out just as for a present-day Legion of Mary Praesidium meeting. There was the white cloth and the statue of the Immaculate Conception, two vases with flowers, two candlesticks with lighted candles — the standard was not there, but otherwise they had the ordinary Legion Altar.

"The Queen was waiting for her soldiers. It is not known who so arranged things. No instructions were given to that effect. It is not suggested that it was miraculously accomplished, but certainly someone was inspired to do it. . . . That remarkable event took place on the 7th of September, 1921. Surely it is rather more than a coincidence that it was the eve of Mary's birthday, that the Legion, then called the Association of Our Lady of Mercy, came into life with the first fragrance of such a feast, that it was really born with Mary!"

The reader reluctantly put aside the story of the Legion. It was getting late, and he must go to Glasnevin cemetery on the morrow to visit Matt's grave. He glanced idly through the pages of the pamphlet about John A. McGuinness, and wondered why he had bought it. At the time it had seemed the right thing to select. Now — what possible connection could McGuinness have with Matt? He threw the little book into his traveling bag. He might have time to read it on the plane.

It was early Sunday afternoon when Miss Morphy and the newspaperman walked through the cemetery gates. The grave was in a quiet corner, about a mile away — a long mile through curving paths bordered by cedars and myrtles. Millions of tiny daisies freckled the grass, and the earth, and the walks — glorious symbols in a mournful world, bright glimpses of eternity showing through the crust of time.

"It's not much farther," Miss Morphy kept saying.

There was a great crowd of people clustered about a grave. The newspaperman thought someone was being buried there, and was for making a detour to avoid the mourners.

"But no," Miss Morphy said. "It's not a funeral at all. It's just the usual Sunday crowd of people come to honor Matt. Let's see if we can get closer. Otherwise you'll not be able to see the grave at all, until the crowd goes, unless you do like Matt did at the dance, crawl through, and pinch the ankles in your way."

They managed to edge nearer. A priest was talking. The newspaperman could hear some of his words distinctly, but not all of them. He was talking of the great privilege God gives the poor. He was talking of the privilege of becoming a saint. He was talking about a poor boy who became Pope Pius X. He was talking of Maria Goretti. He was talking of Matt Talbot.

It was cold, and a nasty rain was gathering in the dull gray skies. But nobody had opened an umbrella, though many had taken them to the cemetery. And scarcely anybody moved. The men's heads were uncovered, as though they were in church. There was an atmosphere of church about the place, of people listening to a sermon between High Mass and Benediction.

The priest was praying for the intentions of the Pope, for peace in the world, for the workers, for those addicted to strong drink. He was asking Matt to pray for all those present, and all their relatives and friends.

Some people left after the priest had finished, and it was easy then to approach the grave. There were still many around it, some just standing there staring at it, some touching Rosaries and scapulars to the headstone, some filling envelopes with soil or pebbles, or sprigs of flowers.

191

"Ever since Matt was buried there," Miss Morphy whispered — there was something in the atmosphere that demanded whispers, reverent whispers—"people have been carrying away envelopes and little bags of earth. They have removed enough clay to make a hole as big as your Grand Canyon. But the grave is just the same. Do you like the flowers?"

There were many beautiful flowers on the grave. There were also several tiny statues of the Little Flower and of the Blessed Virgin.

The reporter was more interested in the people than in the flowers. They made him feel that Matt had been buried only that morning; and that love for him had made all these men and women, strangers to each other, members of one family.

"Is there always such a crowd as this?" he whispered to Miss Morphy.

"In June, yes," was her answer. "Sometimes the crowd is even bigger. People come from North and South America, from Africa, from parts of Asia, from Australia, and from all over Europe. Why is it that sanctity in an ordinary man is so rare that it draws people from all over the earth? Why isn't sanctity the ordinary, the expected, the commonplace, in every one of us Catholics, clerical or lay?"

They knelt, with scores of others, said a prayer or two, and started back toward the gate. Miss Morphy paused at another grave, some little distance from Matt's.

"Let's say a prayer here too," she suggested. "This is another man you would have loved."

They went on again, slowly. "He was an ordinary Catholic," Miss Morphy said. "Just average, you know. Like Matt himself was once. Then one day a friend invited him to make a retreat. He didn't want to go. He tried every way possible to get out of it, but at the last minute, gave in. He promised. And he kept his word. Afterwards, he joined the St. Vincent de Paul Society, and became a much better Catholic than before. A few years later he heard about Matt Talbot. And from that day on he tried to be another Matt. He went to

Matt's sisters and asked for a relic. I think it was Matt's coat he got, or part of it. Maybe the one with the crossed pins in it. It was then the fire of real sanctity began to burn in him."

"Who was he?" the reporter asked. But he knew. He couldn't help knowing. It wasn't mere chance that had put those two pamphlets in his possession. He was sorry he hadn't read both of them.

"His name was Johnny McGuinness," the girl said. She said it with the voice a girl reserves for the name of someone dear to her. "John Anthony McGuinness."

The reporter read the pamphlet (in the skies above the Atlantic). Johnny had been known as "Mac" to his friends. He made the retreat, against his will, in 1924, "early in February." He became a leader in the St. Vincent de Paul Society. In 1932 he found his "greatest zeal and fervour."

"Whatever his previous efforts for the poor and destitute of body and soul may have been," said the author, "I am firmly convinced that the dedication of his life to Almighty God really and truly took place in the midsummer of 1932. Ever after this he conducted himself like a man pledged body and soul to his Redeemer."

The author, who is anonymous, does not mention Matt Talbot; probably he never heard of him. There are still people in Dublin to whom Matt is a stranger. It was in 1932, during the Eucharistic Congress, that the French cardinal visited Matt's room in Upper Rutland Street — and so gave the newspapers an opportunity to mention Matt and bring him to the attention of McGuinness.

It was interesting to note that, "in the middle thirties," Johnny "kept more to himself . . . gave up everything that bordered on luxury . . . had a salary exceeding a thousand pounds a year but lived in a humble flat, cooked his own meals, and spent everything possible on the poor . . . would not spare time to read the papers, or engage in a friendly chat about nothing in particular . . . neither smoked nor drank . . . always neat and scrupulously clean of body, he spent only the bare essentials on his own personal dress — he went to Communion every day . . . never went to cinemas, theaters, dancing halls, card parties, or other entertainments . . . joined the Third Order of St. Francis . . . austere fasts . . . remained a bachelor . . . died penniless."

His last words to a friend were these: "I couldn't do enough for God, no matter what I did. No one could."

Early in February, 1947, almost exactly twenty-three years after he had refused to go to that fateful retreat, and then had changed his mind, John Anthony McGuinness was lowered into the grave not far from that of his pilot and exemplar.

Crowds were still coming into the cemetery, the reporter saw as he reached the gates with Miss Morphy. They were going in the direction of Matt's grave. He remembered Rudolph Valentino, then "the great lover" of the motion-picture world, lying in state on Broadway — Broadway above the bright lights, Broadway above Columbus Circle — and the great crowds waiting in the rain for a chance to file into the undertaker's room and see the body. A mounted police-man tried to keep the crowd in order. They shoved him, and his horse, through a plate-glass window of the mortuary parlor.

Valentino had drawn thousands and thousands of people in that last appearance in New York. He had drawn thousands more when he was buried in a graveyard in California. But then, like other ordinary great mortals, he was neglected and forgotten.

The great lover in Glasnevin was still being visited by friends!

After twenty-seven years, the body he had treated with such rigor and contempt continued to draw men and women pilgrims from all parts of the world.

Yet it wasn't the body that attracted the multitudes. It was the spirit that had animated it, the spirit that other Catholics hoped to find in the vicinity of his grave. Matt had died to himself in life, as a grain of wheat must die if it would bring forth food to feed a hungry world. He had buried that spirit deep in the Sacred Heart. The rich soil had fructified the dead seed, and Mary had tended the plant and brought it to maturity; Mary, the Lady of Fatima, the Bogoroditza of Red Russia, the Sing-Mo-Malya of Red China, the Empress of heaven and earth and the unexplored regions of purgatory.

Matt could be found more readily in the middle of O'Connell Street than in the daisy-spattered grasses of Glasnevin.

Why, the newspaperman wondered, didn't some Catholic lay or hierarchial organization build a shrine of the Sacred Heart, and of Mary, in Washington, D. C., the capital of the United States? and in Ottawa, Ontario, the capital of Canada? And in every other big city in America?

Could there be a better protection for the continent than the blessings with which God would repay the honors Americans had thus rendered Him and His Mother?

But how the devils would rage! The devils without the land, and the devils within.

# 25

LATE in June, 1952, the apostolic process established by the Holy See in the cause of Matt Talbot's beatification and canonization, had completed the examination of witnesses. The tribunal appointed by the archbishop of Dublin had held ninety sessions and carefully questioned twenty-six witnesses under oath.

Whether or not any of the witnesses testified to first-class miracles worked through the intervention of the holy servant of God was not disclosed.

On Sunday, June 29, the body was exhumed, in accordance with canonical procedure; and the archbishop, the Most Rev. John C. McQuaid, issued an official statement, printed here in part.

"The officials who constitute the Tribunal assembled at 10 a.m. in the cemetery chapel, where, after a short prayer, the medical experts took the prescribed oath to fulfill faithfully the office entrusted to them and to give a true and accurate report concerning their examination of the body of

196

the Servant of God, the state of preservation, and any other circumstances about which information might be required by the Tribunal. The special witnesses called to identify the grave likewise took an oath to speak the truth in their testimony.

"All present then walked to the grave, which is described in the cemetery records as 'No. SK 319½, St. Bridget's section, Prospect Cemetery, Glasnevin.' The grave was well kept and had some fresh flowers. On Saturday evening a wreath had been placed there and bore the inscription: 'From the Matt Talbot League. Deo Gratias.'

"The coffin of the Servant of God, when opened, revealed his mortal remains in skeleton form, and the burial shroud, which appeared to be a Franciscan Habit. In the coffin were also found three chains, one large and two smaller, three large medals, two crucifixes, and portions of a large Rosary Beads. . . .

"When the remains of the Servant of God had been removed from the grave and set in a specially-prepared new coffin, they were carried in procession to the cemetery chapel. The old coffin, pieces of clay found therein, and what remained of the shroud, were placed in a separate box and brought to the chapel. There the medical experts, having carefully examined and re-assembled the parts of the body, secured the bones with strong thread on a white silk cloth.

"His Grace, the Archbishop, in the presence of the distinguished ecclesiastical and lay visitors, invited for the occasion, then recited the prayer for the Beatification of Matt Talbot. Very Rev. T. O'Donnell, vice-postulator of the Cause, read the formal decree of excommunication that would be incurred by anyone who would dare to remove any portion of the remains or precious relics of the servant of God which lay upon the altar. Each witness reverently viewed the remains and relics and signed the formal parchment of attestation.

"Later the President (of Ireland), Mr. Sean T. O'Kelly, who had returned from Donegal specially to be present at

Glasnevin, was introduced by the Archbishop and paid his respects to the Servant of God and signed the parchment.

"This document, having been signed, sealed, and dated by His Grace, the Archbishop, was enclosed in a metal case which was likewise sealed and later placed in the new coffin as proof of the authenticity of the remains.

"The medical report which had been made under oath and signed, was duly witnessed, and will be inserted in the Acts of the Process.

"When the remains of the Servant of God, the smaller pieces of bone, and the metal case had been placed in the new coffin, this coffin was closed with six screws, and each screw was sealed by His Grace, the Archbishop. This coffin was in turn enclosed in a larger and stronger oak coffin, and on each of the two straps joining the coffins were placed by His Grace two further seals. The brass plate on the other coffin bears the simple inscription: 'The Servant of God, Matthew Talbot.'

"The coffin was then borne in procession by the grave-diggers to the vault prepared. Before the coffin walked the Officials of the Tribunal. . . . Over the iron gate of the vault is a marble plaque inscribed: 'Servant of God Matthew Talbot,' and attached to the gate of the vault is a framed copy of the prayer for beatification. . . .

"The ceremony of exhumation brings to an end the investigations ordered to be made by the Apostolic Process. It is to be noted that the ceremony is a necessary part of the Process and does not anticipate any decision of the Holy See. The complete Acts of the Process, when they have been transcribed in proper form, will be transmitted to the Sacred Congregation of Rites of the Holy See."

Sometime after Matt's body had been placed in the vault, the American heard from two friends across the sea.

"I went to the cemetery on the Saturday before the great day," Miss Morphy wrote, "with all the working girls who make up the 'Matt Talbot Missionary Workers.' They had presented a bouquet of roses, lilies, and carnations. I tied it

198

up with a wide satin ribbon and cellophane. This is the bouquet mentioned in the official statement from the Archbishop. On Monday, when we went up to the vault, the flowers had been placed on the new coffin. I was thrilled to think we were last with Matt at the grave and first at the vault.

"All that Saturday before the exhumation, crowds had paid a last visit to the grave. Many had placed great bunches of flowers there. Some had just laid them on the earth. Others were removing old leaves, weeds, soil, and stones. Surely everyone had guessed why the cemetery was to be closed the following day.

"The bell rang to notify us that the gates were to be closed; but I could not leave. I knew I had lost my job of decorating the grave, which I had done every Sunday, especially during June, since 1932. Crowds visit the vault every day. The heavy door is open, but there is an iron grill to look through. The coffin is quite near the door but not near enough to touch with your hand.

"One man opened the laces of his boot, tied his Rosary to it, swung it through the opening, and touched the coffin.

"The crowds come down to Granby Lane too. I'm afraid our 'visitors' book is not produced all the time these days. It would be filled up too soon."

And Mrs. Sweeney wrote: "Matt is no longer in the clay. He's in a beautiful vault. I saw his sanctified remains being conveyed in a pontifically sealed oak coffin, surrounded by the pontifical judges of the court, in their magnificent robes of scarlet and red, conveyed from and to the mortuary chapel.

"I was outside the gates of the cemetery from early morning 'til 7:30 p.m., and the scene was one never to be effaced from my memory. I cannot describe to you fully my feeling of ecstatic joy at the phenomenal progress made in Matt's Cause, for which, during most of my life, I have labored.

"It only remains for us to ask the Great Master in heaven

to bring Matt to the golden gates of the canonized. God bless you."

\* \* \*

How long will it be before Matt is beatified — if he is to be so honored? The Very Rev. Gerard Oesterle, O.S.B., postulator for the cause of Sister Mary Fortunata Viti, O.S.B., an Italian nun, states that at the present time there are 1200 "such processes" moving through the Roman courts.

"These cases," he says, "must wait their respective turns on the docket, and these turns cannot come around very often, considering the limited number of sessions a court can hold in a year's time."

Well, Matt is used to waiting. He used to wait hours for the pub to open. He used to wait hours for the doors of a church to open. He waited years for the gates of heaven to open and let him slake his thirst for Love. He can wait for the honors of the Church. And — he's in good company.